Wild Cat Species of the World

Richard Green

Basset Publications
Plymouth

Acknowledgements

The author and publishers gratefully acknowledge and thank the following for supplying photographs:-

The Onza - Courtesy of the International Society of Cryptozoology, Tucson, Arizona, USA.

Pallas's Cat - Ed. Nazarov and Sergei V. Popov, Moscow Zoo, 123820, B. Gruzinskaya, 1 USSR.

Geoffroy's Cat- Courtesy of Steve A. Clevenger, The Birmingham Zoo, Birmingham, Alabama, USA.

Rusty Spotted Cat, Ocelot, Puma, European Wildcat - Courtesy of Ray Charter, Freelance Photographer, London.

In addition the author would like to thank virtually every cat keeper in the United Kingdom, they have all, either wittingly or unwittingly, assisted in his researches. Grateful thanks are also due to the author's wife, Edna, without whom the whole project would have foundered on the sands.

First Published October 1991

I.S.B.N. 0 946873 93 3

Published by Basset Publications, 60, North Hill, Plymouth, S. Devon.

Printed by The Western Litho Company of Plymouth, Heather House, Gibbon Lane, Plymouth, S. Devon.

Front cover: Puma - courtesy of Ray Charter

CONTENTS

1	General Description	1
2	European Wild Cat	4
3	African Wild Cat	9
4	Domestic Cat	13
5	Sand Cat	16
6	Jungle Cat	19
7	Black-footed Cat	22
8	Chinese Desert Cat	26
9	Serval	28
10	Caracal	32
11	Lynx	36
12	Spanish Lynx	41
13	Bobcat	44
14	Pallas's Cat	49
15	Leopard Cat	52
16	Rusty-spotted Cat	56
17	Fishing Cat	58
18	Iriomote Cat	61
19	Flat-Headed Cat	63
20	African Golden Cat	65
21	Temminck's Cat	68
22	Bay Cat	71
23	Jaguarundi	73
24	Ocelot	76
25	Margay	80

26	Oncilla	84
27	Geoffroy's Cat	86
28	Kodkod	90
29	Pampas Cat	92
30	Andean Cat	95
31	Puma	97
32	Marbled Cat	103
33	Clouded Leopard	106
34	Snow Leopard	110
35	Leopard	115
36	Jaguar	121
37	Tiger	125
38	Lion	131
39	Cheetah	138
40	Onza	144
	Bibliography	146
	Index	162

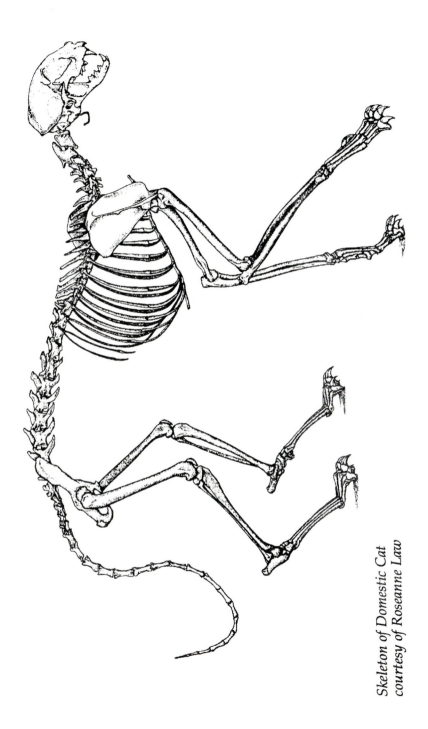

Skeleton of Domestic Cat
courtesy of Roseanne Law

Chapter One

A GENERAL DESCRIPTION

Cats as a group are very much alike. They have a short muzzle compared with that of a dog. The ears are set high on the head and the skull frequently has a rounded shape. The eyes have a well developed membrane which can be pulled across to clean the surface of the conjunctiva. There is a reflecting layer in the eyes called the tapetum which may have some function in amplifying the light received by the eye. The sensitivity of a cats eye is such that it can distinguish levels c illumination far below that which man is capable of. This may be the origin of the saying that cats can see in the dark.

The pupils of most cats eyes close to a slit in daylight but there are some that close symmetrically to a pinprick. Cats eyes have been shown to have both green absorbing and blue absorbing cones which gives them the ability to distinguish most of the spectrum. Research has not yet revealed the presence of red absorbing cones but it is possible that they exist.

The vibrissae or whiskers transmit tactile information to the nervous system. They consist of areas of long bristles on either side of the muzzle, a tuft above the eyes, another in front of the ears, and yet another just in front of the hinge of the mandible.

The hearing of the cat is sensitive to high frequency sound but the sensitivity decreases with age. This sensitivity to high frequency could be useful when hunting small prey. It is possibly significant that those species that live in areas of long grass tend to have larger ears in comparison to the size of the body. It has been shown that cats are capable of distinguishing between sounds that are separated by less than a semi-tone. It has also been demonstrated that the pencil tufts on the ears of some species aid in pin-pointing the location of a sound and that animals that are deprived of them are handicapped in their hunting.

The skeleton of the cat consists of 230 bones compared to the 206 found in man. The teeth normally number 30 although a few species have 28. The teeth always appear in a fixed sequence. The deciduous incisors usually appear in the first two weeks and are followed in the third week by the canines. The premolar teeth appear between the fourth week and the ninth week. The deciduous incisors are shed between the ages of three and a half and five and a half months at which time the permanent incisors appear. The premolars are replaced at between four and six months of age. The molars erupt between four and a half and five and a half months of age and during the following month the deciduous canines are replaced by the permanent ones. These timings refer to the domestic cat, timings for other species, where known, are given in the text.

Cats have several sets of glands which they use to mark objects and points within their territory for the purpose of communicating with other cats. Firstly there are the temporal glands which are situated on each side of the forehead, these are frequently used for initial marking. This is followed by marking with the peri-oral glands which are situated along the lips. The anal glands are situated on either side of and slightly below the anus, and finally there are the caudal glands which are situated along the tail. Owners of domestic cats will be familiar with the way in which they rub themselves with their whole length around the owners legs. Cats, when checking a scent deposit, may exhibit the facial reaction known as 'flehmen', this is done by curling back the upper lid in an exaggerated manner, The purpose of this may be to ensure that the scent reaches the Jacobson's organ on the roof of the mouth in order to be more easily identified.

The ears of the cat give a very good indication of the mood that it is in, if the ears are upright the cat is at rest and in an amiable mood. If the cat is making a defensive threat the ears are flattened outwards from the head with the backs showing, an offensive threat is signalled by the ears in an upright position and being rotated to show the backs. When the cat is about to attack the ears are flattened backwards towards the neck so that they almost disappear.

The main difference between big cats and small cats lies in the composition of the hyoid arch, (the structure which supports the larynx). In small cats it is composed completely of bone, this inhibits the working of the larynx so that they are able to purr continuously; it also makes their voices high pitched screams. In big cats the hyoid is composed partly of cartilage, this means that the movement of the larynx is not restricted thus enabling the big cats to roar, it also means that they must take a fresh breath between each exhalation if they wish to purr.

Another slight, but significant, difference between big and small cats is that small cats have a strip of skin across the end of the muzzle just above the nostrils, this is known as the nose leather. On big cats the fur comes right up to the nostrils.

Recent research reveals that all cat species have the same complement of genes to control the colour variations of the coat. There appear to be about ten genes involved, these genes and their mutations account for all the colour variations observed in cats.

The exact classification of the cat family is in a state of turmoil. Therefore the best that one can do is to follow the system established by one taxonomist. In this text the classification system described by Hemmer (1978) will be followed in the main; the order of the species has been altered slightly in order to place related species closer to each other in the listing.

Chapter Two

EUROPEAN WILD CAT
Felis sylvestris Schreber 1777

Vital Statistics

Length	head and body	47.5 - 75 cm.
	tail	26 - 37 cm.
Height at shoulder		35 - 40 cm.
Weight		3 - 8 kg.
Age of Maturity		11 months
Dental formula		$I\,^3/_3$ $C\,^1/_1$ $P\,^3/_2$ $M\,^1/_1$
Chromosome number		38
Karyotype		1 (Robinson)
Longevity		up to 15 years
Gestation period		63 - 68 days
Number of young		1 - 8
Weight at birth		80 - 135 g.
Young weaned		3 - 4 months

Description

This cat is larger and heavier than the Domestic Cat, it is also more stockily built; it has a broad head, wide set ears and a blunt bushy tail. The face and head have distinct tabby markings, the nose leather is flesh coloured and the throat is white. The ground colour of the coat is yellow-brownish grey being darker on the back and becoming very pale on the underside. There is a broad black dorsal stripe from which transverse stripes run in an irregular manner to the belly, the tail has black encircling bands and a black tip. There are also black bands on the legs. Kittens are more strongly marked than their parents and for the first few months of their lives they have a tapered tail. The female normally has four pairs of teats.

Distribution

The Wild Cat is found from the Caspian Sea westward to the Atlantic Ocean. The southern boundary of the range is formed by the Mediterranean Sea and includes Asia Minor. The northern boundary of the range runs through Poland and Czechoslovakia, it then runs through Germany, being found as far North as the Eifel region, the boundary then runs through the French

Alps into Spain. The species is also found in Scotland but is no longer found in Scandinavia.

Habitat

The Wild Cat is primarily a creature of the deciduous forests but it is very adaptable and so can be found in open, though rocky terrain. In some parts of its range it will visit heaths, moorlands and marsh lands, individuals have been known to settle in such country. The species also inhabits scrubland of the type known as 'maquis', in some places it will even live in pine forest, though this is normally a comparatively sterile environment.

Habits

The Wild Cat is at its most active in the morning and the evening, at which times it does most of its hunting. When it is seen out during the day it is usually sunning itself. Hunting seldom takes place at night. The prey of the Wild Cat consists mostly of rodents which makes this species a good friend of the farmer. Although they will generally shun water they have been seen eating fish and migrating eels when the latter are on their way overland. Hares, grouse and the young of some species of deer form a small part of their diet, and when desperate, they will eat carrion and the refuse of man.

For most of the year the Wild Cat is a solitary animal with males and females holding separate territories which they mark with scent posts and scratching. As long as food is plentiful they will stick rigidly to the territory, but they will leave it to wander far and wide when food is scarce or in order to find a mate. The size of the territory varies with the type of country, as an example in the Carpathian forests it is about 2.5 square miles while in other places it may be as much as twice this size. Within this territory there are several places where the cat has a den or a favourite resting place. The majority of these places are on the ground because, although Wild Cats will take to the trees when pursued, they are essentially a ground dwelling animal.

The vocalizations of the Wild Cat are very much the same as those of the Domestic Cat with the proviso that the agonistic sounds are louder and uttered with very much more venom than those of the Domestic Cat. In spite of the reports of its ferocity the author has found it to be no more fierce than any other species of animal.

Apart from man the enemies of the Wild Cat are principally the Lynx, the Fox, and the Eagle, although there are stories of Wild Cat killing Eagles.

Breeding

Mating takes place in February and March and is accompanied by the vocalisation familiar to those who have heard 'alley-cats' in the cities. Several males will approach a female at once and will make loud howling noises while they are doing so, sometimes fights will break out. The female greets them with hissing of surprising venom, spitting and unearthly yells. When the female has made her choice she crouches in front of the male who mounts her, at the moment of mating he bites the back of her neck and she frequently turns on him with a snarl. Mating is repeated frequently throughout the oestrous period which lasts five days or so.

The kittens which usually number two or three are born between the middle of April and the middle of May in a den made in a hollow tree, a rocky cave, or the abandoned burrow of another species. If for any reason the litter is lost the female will mate again as little as ten days later, kittens born after conception at this time may have given rise to the stories of Wild Cats being able to breed throughout the year.

Development of Young

The kittens are born blind and their eyes open between seven and twelve days of age. They start to lift their body weight clear of the ground at about two and a half weeks and will begin to leave the den at about five weeks. Observations on captive animals where the male is still at large and able to hunt have indicated that the male will bring food back to the den for the female and kittens. When the kittens start leaving the den the female will start to bring back live prey for them to practice hunting with. While the kittens are suckling the mother adopts a sitting position, as if in an armchair, and the young lie up in her lap.

6

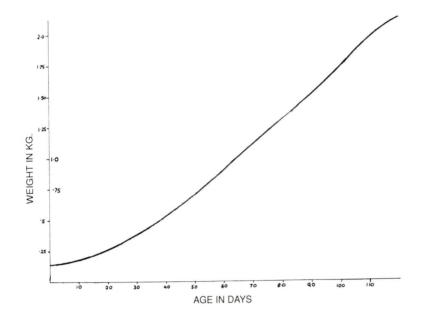

Average weight gain in European Wild Cat Kittens

Kittens start to accompany their mother on hunting expeditions when they are about ten or twelve weeks old. By the beginning of their first winter the kittens are independent and it is very likely that at this time there is a high level of mortality amongst them. It appears that they reach maturity at about one year old, although it is possible that they do not breed until they are at least two years old.

The full development of deciduous dentition is reached at about six or seven weeks.

Status and Systematics

In spite of having official protection the Wild Cat is persecuted by man throughout its range despite the good it does in controlling rodents. Consequently it must be regarded as vulnerable, and locally as being rare. In Scotland it is slowly increasing its numbers and extending its range.

The European Wild Cat is the type species for the Genus *Felis* and is the most well known to the layman. It varies a little throughout its range and is generally considered to have seven sub-species.

The International Species Indexing System numbers are as follows:-

1412007001026	European Wild Cat File Number	
1412007001026001	*Felis sylvestris*	General entry
1412007001026002	*Felis sylvestris sylvestris*	Central Europe - South West Russia
1412007001026003	*Felis sylvestris caucasia*	Asia Minor
1412007001026004	*Felis sylvestris euxina*	Romania
1412007001026005	*Felis sylvestris grampia*	Scotland
1412007001026006	*Felis sylvestris molisana*	Italy
1412007001026007	*Felis sylvestris morea*	South Greece
1412007001026008	*Felis sylvestris tartesia*	South Spain

Chapter Three

AFRICAN WILD CAT
Felis lybica Forster 1780

Vital Statistics

Length	head and body	55 - 65 cm.
	tail	30 - 35 cm.
Height at Shoulder		35.5 cm.
Weight		approx. 5.5 kg.
Age at maturity		approx. 11 months
Dental formula		$I^3/_3 \quad C^1/_1 \quad P^3/_2 \quad M^1/_1$
Chromosome count		38
Karyotype		1 (Robinson)
Longevity		15 years
Gestation period		56 - 63 days
Number of young		1 - 5
Weight at birth		100 - 120 g.
Young weaned		3 - 4 months

Description

In contrast to the European Wild Cat this species has a tapering tail and the ground colour of the coat varies from a pale reddish tinge to a full dark grey colour, all intermediate shades are found. Markings range from black to brown in colour, in the far East of the range the markings are very faint whilst in other places it is almost indistinguishable from a 'tabby' coloured Domestic Cat. Stripes run over the top of the head, and also run from the dorsal line to the belly. In some individuals the stripes are broken into spots, the fore legs and upper hind legs have very dark bands around them. The backs of the ears are sometimes black although they can be almost any of the principal coat shades. There is a great deal of colour variation throughout the range, darker individuals tend to be found in humid forest regions and lighter individuals in dry country. This is the species that is known in Africa as the Caffer Cat. The female normally has four pairs of teats.

Distribution

The African Wild Cat is distributed over all of Africa and also over large parts of Asia. It is present in Mongolia and in the

Western Steppes extending as far as the East and South shores of the Caspian Sea. It is also found in Pakistan, Afghanistan and Arabia, but not in Tibet.

Habitat

Similar to the European Wild Cat, this species will inhabit many different types of country, possibly it shows a greater tolerance for harsh conditions than the previous species. The only habitats that it appears to truly shun are tropical rain forest and desert.

Habits

Like the European Wild Cat this species is solitary in its habits and is mainly a nocturnal hunter, although in cloudy or dull weather it can be seen hunting by day. During the day it usually hides in cover such as hollow trees, thickets or rocky crevices. It does not avoid man to the same extent as its European cousin, and often lives close to villages and farms.

Generally the presence of this species near farms is welcomed by man because it helps to keep down the rodent population. In fact most of the food of this cat consists of rodents although it will also eat hares, snakes, lizards, large insects and birds up to the size of Guinea Fowl. During a drought in Oman one cat is known to have survived on dates, beetles and grasshoppers. Similarly in Kazakhstan the Wild Cat has been recorded as eating the berries of the Russian Olive Tree and the Nitre Bush.

The vocalisations of this species are to all intents and purposes the same as those of the Domestic Cat. While the Wild Cat is primarily terrestrial it is also a good climber and will take to the trees not only to avoid potential danger but also to effect ambush.

Breeding

It is not known if the Wild Cat is a seasonal breeder throughout its range, it is however known to come into oestrous in January and February in Central Asia. Captive individuals in Europe have also shown oestrous in Spring. Oestrous lasts for about four days and is accompanied by loud vocalisations. The gestation period is shorter than that of the European Wild Cat but otherwise the breeding is similar.

Development of Young

The kittens (usually two or three) are born blind and their eyes open at about ten or eleven days old. They start to leave the nest at about four weeks of age and begin to eat solid food at about five weeks. Physical growth is rapid, male kittens reach the same height as their mothers when they are five months old, from then on however growth slows so that they reach mature proportions at about three years. Permanent teeth are all acquired by the age of five and a half months.

Status and Systematics

In Southern Africa this species is locally common, whilst in North Africa, Arabia and Pakistan it is becoming rare. In Central Asia it is locally abundant, possibly this is because the nature of the terrain it lives in secures it from persecution.

The African Wild Cat is generally assumed to be the ancestor of the Domestic Cat, indeed it is more easily tameable than the European Wild Cat, however some authorities consider the European African forms to belong to the same species.

There are considered to be twenty one sub-species of the African Wild Cat, two of these were formerly thought to be sub-species of the Chinese Desert Cat.

The International Species Indexing System numbers are as follows:-

1412007001014	African Wild Cat File Number	
1412007001014001	*Felis libyca*	General Entry
1412007001014002	*Felis libyca libyca*	Morocco to Egypt
1412007001014003	*Felis libyca brockmani*	Somalia
1412007001014004	*Felis libyca cafra*	Rep. of South Africa
1412007001014005	*Felis libyca caudata*	Turkey to Iran, Afghanistan
1412007001014006	*Felis libyca foxi*	Guinea to Cameroon
1412007001014007	*Felis libyca griselda*	North Botswana, Namibia
1412007001014008	*Felis libyca iraki*	Arabia and Iraq
1412007001014009	*Felis libyca issikulensis*	East Russia, Turkistan

1412007001014010	*Felis libyca koslowi*	East Tienshan Mountains
1412007001014011	*Felis libyca matschiei*	Transcaucasia
1412007001014012	*Felis libyca mellandi*	Malawi, East Zambia
1412007001014013	*Felis libyca murgabensis*	Afghan-Turkestan border
1412007001014014	*Felis libyca nesterovi*	Iraq and South Iran
1412007001014015	*Felis libyca ocreata*	Ethiopia
1412007001014016	*Felis libyca ornata*	North and Central India
1412007001014017	*Felis libyca pyrrhus*	South Angola
1412007001014018	*Felis libyca rubida*	Sudan to Tanzania
1412007001014019	*Felis libyca sarda*	Mediterranean Isles, North Africa
1412007001014020	*Felis libyca tristami*	Syria, Aden, Saudi Arabia
1412007001004003	*Felis libyca chutuchta*	South Mongolia
1412007001004004	*Felis libyca vellerosa*	North East Shansi

Chapter Four

DOMESTIC CAT
Felis catus Linnaeus 1758

Vital Statistics

Length	head and body	approx. 40 cm.
	tail	approx. 25 cm.
Height at shoulder		approx. 30 cm.
Weight		4 - 8 kg.
Dental formula		$I^3/_3$ $C^1/_1$ $P^3/_2$ $M^1/_1$
Chromosome count		38
Karyotype		1 (Robinson)
Longevity		25 years (rare cases)
Gestation Period		63 - 68 days
Number of young		1 - 8
Weight at birth		approx. 90 g.
Age weaned		approx. 8 weeks

Description

The Domestic Cat exhibits a variety of coat colours, it can also have either long or short hair, and can be with or without pencil tufts on the ears. The nose leather has a variety of colours. The feet likewise may have long hairs between the pads or not. These variations result in the Domestic Cat having a large number of forms which in the case of this species are known as breeds.

When the Domestic Cat leaves human habitation and becomes feral the colour which tends to predominate is that which is known as 'tabby', however a study of English dockyard cats revealed that the colour most likely to survive in that environment was black. The female normally has four pairs of teats.

Distribution

The Domestic Cat has through the influence of man been spread worldwide, with the exception of the Polar regions there is almost no corner of the Earth where it is not found.

Habitat

Where the Domestic Cat leaves the dwelling of man and leads a feral life it usually sticks to woodland, but not dense forest, or to heath and scrubland. Feral cats also keep to a farmland environment and do a good job by keeping rodents in check.

Habits

Left to themselves Domestic Cats are solitary and nocturnal. Hunting is carried out usually at dawn and dusk or is accomplished by locating the prey by scent, sight or sound, then stalking it and pouncing on the victim. Prey is frequently killed by a bite to the nape of the neck.

Marking of the territory is carried out by both males and females using the glands situated around the body. The male also marks by spraying very strong smelling urine onto convenient objects near the perimeter of his territory. The marking by the female, as well as indicating the extent of her territory to other cats, also indicates to nearby males whether or not she is in oestrous.

Cats on farms usually have a bigger territory than those which live in towns, the country cat may range as much as a kilometre from its base and have a regular, well trod, beat. Town cats are more likely to be seen in close quarters than are their country cousins, they will gather wherever there is an abundance of food, or several males may gather when pursuing a female.

Breeding

A female may become sexually mature at between six to eight months old but a male does not exhibit mating behaviour until about ten months. Feral and farm cats keep close to a wild cat form of oestrous cycle, having a litter in the spring and, if this is lost, another in early summer. House cats will mate and give birth at almost any time of the year.

The female that is in oestrous paces a great deal, indulges in frequent bouts of head rubbing and starts calling, the calling reaches a crescendo as the oestrous approaches its peak. Males will come from far and wide to seek a female in oestrous, and several will square up to each other to decide the battle for supremacy and the female. It is usually the female who makes the choice of mate, she crouches in front of the chosen male who then mounts her. During mating the cats may make crooning noises to each other. Immediately after mating the male jumps back out of the way as the female usually turns to attack him with tooth and claw. Mating takes place frequently during oestrous and has been observed to be as often as ten times per hour.

The composition of maternal milk is as follows:-

Water	82.35%
Fat	4.95%
Protein	7.15%
Carhbohydrate	4.90%
Ash	0.65%

Development of Young

The kittens are born blind and their eyes open at between two and ten days old, at around three weeks the kittens are able to stand and move about. At approximately four or five weeks the feral or farm cat will change the kittens to another nest. The female will teach the kittens to play by enticing them with the end of her tail. By the time that they are six weeks old the kittens are playing chasing games and by the age of three months the hunting instinct is very well developed, together with a propensity to investigate every new situation, place or opportunity.

Growth stops at about ten months, although the female may put on weight after her first litter.

Systematics

The Domestic Cat has a large number of varieties or breeds, however since these are considered to have been created by selective breeding they are not recognised as sub-species.

The International Species Indexing System numbers are:-

1412007001006	Domestic Cat File Number	
1412007001006001	*Felis catus*	Worldwide

Chapter Five

SAND CAT
Felis margarita Loche 1858

Vital Statistics

Length	head and body				48 - 58 cm.
	tail				28 - 35 cm.
Height at Shoulder					approx. 25 cm.
Weight					3 - 4 kg.
Age at maturity					14 months
Dental formula	$I^3/_3$	$C^1/_1$	$P^3/_2$	$M^1/_1$	
Chromosome count					38
Karyotype					1 (Robinson)
Longevity					up to 8 years
Gestation period					60 - 63 days
Number of young					1 - 8
Weight at birth					approx. 39 g.

Description

The Sand Cat is a small cat with short legs, having a wide flattish head with large ears set low and long cheek fur. The pelt is soft and thick with a ground colour that varies from sandy to straw ochre, the shading being darker on the back and paler on the underside. A reddish stripe runs from the outer corners of the eyes across the cheeks and there are blackish bars on the legs. The backs of the ears are tawny tipped with black, the tail also is tipped with black and has two or three tawny rings around it. The soles of the feet are covered with a dense mat of hairs which completely cover the pads and protect the feet from scorching sand. The middle ear cavity of this species is extremely large and indicates that most of the hunting is done by sound. The young are more strongly marked than their parents.

Distribution and Habitat

The Sand Cat, as its name suggests, is a desert dweller and is found in the Sahara, Sinai and Arabian deserts in the Western part of its range. It is also found in the Karakum, Kizilkum and Patakum deserts of Central Asia and the Nushki desert of West

Pakistan. The species inhabits extremely arid areas where there are sand-dunes with small desert dwelling plants to provide cover, and also rocky areas.

Habits

The Sand Cat is exclusively terrestrial in its habits, the greater part of its activity starting at dusk. Rodents, particularly gerbils, form the bulk of the prey although birds, lizards and arthropods are also eaten. This species appears to be capable of living without access to open water for drinking.

In the heat of the day they lie up in shallow burrows dug at the base of shrubs or small mounds, since gerbils are active by day we can assume that for at least some of the time Sand Cats are active by day. Sand Cats appear to spend a great deal of time digging, either making burrows or looking for subterranean rodents.

The vocalizations of the Sand Cat seem to be very much the same as those of the Domestic Cat, however one call not found in that species is one uttered by the male which consists of a loud barking similar to that of a small dog. This call combined with the cats sharpness of hearing may enable individuals to keep in touch with each other in the featureless habitat of the desert.

Breeding and Development of the Young

In some parts of its range the Sand Cat seems to give birth in April or May, however in captivity young have been born at all times of the year. Although little studied it may be presumed that the courting behaviour of the Sand Cat broadly follows the pattern of other species. The size of the litter can be as many as eight, the mean size being four. The kittens are born blind and at birth weigh about 39g. Their weight increases by about 12g. per day for the first three weeks. Their eyes open at twelve to sixteen days. They start to show digging behaviour at about five weeks old and in the wild leave the family at about seven or eight months of age.

Status and Systematics

Everywhere throughout its range the Sand Cat is rare and in Pakistan it is regarded as being endangered.

There are usually considered to be five sub-species although consideration is being given to raising the Arabian form to separate sub-specific rank.

The International Species Indexing Systems numbers are as follows:-

1412007001017	Sand Cat File Number	
1412007001017001	*Felis margarita*	General entry
1412007001017002	*Felis margarita margarita*	Algeria to Arabia
1412007001017003	*Felis margarita airensis*	Niger
1412007001017004	*Felis margarita meinertzhageni*	Sahara
1412007001017005	*Felis margarita thinobius*	Russian Turkestan
1412007001017006	*Felis margarita scheffeli*	Pakistan

Chapter Six

JUNGLE CAT, SWAMP CAT, REED CAT
Felis chaus Güldenstaedt 1776

Vital Statistics

Length	head and body	60 - 75 cm.
	tail	22 - 29 cm.
Height at shoulder		35 - 38 cm.
Weight		7.25 - 16 kg.
Dental formula		$I\,^3/_3$ $C\,^1/_1$ $P\,^3/_2$ $M\,^1/_1$
Chromosome count		38
Karyotype		1 (Robinson)
Longevity		approx. 14 years
Gestation period		63 - 68 days
Number of young		1 - 7
Age weaned		14 - 16 weeks

Description

This cat is medium sized, strongly built with relatively long legs, a short tail and small pencil tufts on the ears, which themselves are fairly large. At first sight this species is a uniform colour all over but, on closer inspection it can be seen to have markings, which, though faint are of a darker colour than the rest of the coat. The ground colour of the coat varies from sandy grey in the North of the range to tawny red in the South and East. There are faint bars at the top of the legs and bands around the tail which has a black tip. There are indistinct spots on the bodies of some individuals. The tip of the ear is black. There is also a very faint 'tear stain' stripe on the face which is often lighter in colour than the rest of the cat. The kittens when born have very distinct 'tabby' markings and are coloured black and grey. This baby coat is lost by the time they are six months old. Melanistic specimens have been recorded both in the wild and in captivity.

Distribution and Habitat

This species is found in Lower Egypt, Israel, the Middle East (except the Arabian Peninsula) from Asia Minor to Turkestan,

19

India, Burma, Sri Lanka, Indo-China and possibly also Yunnan in China.

The Jungle Cat inhabits thickets, reed beds, open grass lands and even places where there are arable crops. It has been found from sea level up to 2,400 metres above sea level in the Himalayas. In places it will even live in open forest and in Kashmir has been known to take shelter in buildings. The only habitats that this cat appears to avoid are dense rain forest and desert.

Habits

The Jungle Cat is mostly diurnal in its activity pattern and is principally terrestrial. Individuals hold a territory which they mark by spraying trees and prominent places on the boundaries. Within their territory they have several dens which are usually in the disused burrow of another species such as badger, fox or porcupine; sometimes the den may be amongst reeds or under a bush.

Jungle Cats commonly move at a trot, but are capable of moving at up to twenty-three kilometres per hour when necessary. When provoked they can be very aggressive. Although they are good at climbing they seldom venture up trees preferring, when they must, to jump, which they can do up to a considerable height.

The prey consists mostly of rats, mice, lizards and frogs, they are also known to kill porcupines and hares. They are a potential predator on the fawns of Axis Deer *(Axis axis)*. Like all cats they are great opportunists when it comes to feeding and probably they eat birds and other animals a great deal more frequently than previously thought.

Breeding

In the wild the Jungle Cat appears to vary its breeding season according to the latitude of its home. For instance in India they do not appear to have a fixed breeding season, whilst in Russian territory, East of the Caucasus they breed in February and March, but not until April in Turkestan. In captivity Jungle Cats will breed all year round.

During courtship the male pursues the female sniffing to test her readiness to mate. The oestrous lasts five or six days and is accompanied by a magnified version of the type of vocalizations used by the Domestic Cat.

The kittens, usually three or four in number, are born in a concealed dry site such as a nest in a reed bed lined with fur. Other recorded dens have been under rocks and in the abandoned burrows of other species. A captive female exhibited oestrous forty-six days after the birth of her previous litter.

Systematics

In spite of its Lynx like appearance the Jungle Cat is more closely related to the Wild Cats and is therefore included in the Genus *Felis*. There are generally considered to be nine subspecies.

The International Species Indexing System numbers are as follows:

1412007001007	Jungle Cat File Number	
1412007001007001	*Felis chaus*	General Entry
1412007001007002	*Felis chaus chaus*	Turkestan - Iran Baluchistan
1412007001007003	*Felis chaus affinis*	Kashmir Sikkim Yunnan
1412007001007004	*Felis chaus fulvidina*	Indo-China, Burma Thailand
1412007001007005	*Felis chaus furax*	South Syria, Iraq
1412007001007006	*Felis chaus kelaarti*	Sri Lanka, South India
1412007001007007	*Felis chaus kutas*	Bengal - Kutch
1412007001007008	*Felis chaus nilotica*	Egypt
1412007001007009	*Felis chaus oxiana*	Russia
1412007001007010	*Felis chaus prateri*	West India

Chapter Seven

BLACK-FOOTED CAT
Felis nigripes Burchell 1822

Vital Statistics

Length	head and body	male 42 - 50 cm.
		female 33 - 37 cm.
	tail	male 15 - 20 cm.
		female 15 - 17 cm.
Height at shoulder		approx. 25 cm.
Weight		male 2.5 kg. female 1.6 kg.
Age at maturity		approx. 21 months
Dental formula		$I\,^3/_3$ $C\,^1/_1$ $P\,^3/_2$ $M\,^1/_1$
Chromosome count		38
Karyotype		1 (Robinson)
Longevity		approx. 13 years
Gestation period		63 - 68 days
Number of young		1 - 3
Weight at birth		60 - 90 g.

Description

The Black-footed Cat is smaller than a Domestic Cat and is often considered to be the smallest cat in the world, a distinction for which it has rivals in both South America and Asia. The ground colour of the coat varies from dark ochre to sandy grey being darker on the back and lighter on the belly. On the coat there are elongated spots which vary from brown to black, depending upon the individual, on the shoulders these are arranged in rows which merge together into stripes. The soles of the feet are black, giving the cat its name, the legs are short and there are black bars on the forelegs. The tail is short and is ringed with black bands, the ears are rounded and have pale brown backs. The female normally has three pairs of teats.

Distribution and Habitat

This species is limited to the Southern part of the African continent, it is present in Botswana, and in Namibia as far West as Okahandja. In Cape Province it occurs as far South as Fort Beaufort and spreads East into the Orange Free State, Transvaal and Zimbabwe. Its presence has been confirmed in the Kruger National Park. Within this range the Black-footed Cat prefers dry types of country ranging from sandy semi-desert to grassy savannah.

Habits

Observations in the Kruger National Park indicate that this cat follows a crepuscular lifestyle and in captivity it is found to be more diurnal than most cats. It makes its den in the burrows of jumping hares and other animals, often taking over hollow termite hills, this practice has earned the cat the nick-name 'ant-hill tiger'. It is probable that the range of prey includes ground squirrels, small rodents, birds and small reptiles; it has also been reported to kill sheep, this, if true, indicates that it could also kill small antelope. They commonly dig for ants and other insects and appear to have a large appetite for grass.

From the patrolling habits of captive specimens it can be surmised that the male has a larger territory than the female and that the male marks the territory by spraying.

Vocalizations are the same as the Wild Cat with two interesting additions; when danger has passed a mother will signal to her kittens the 'all clear' by means of a staccato noise which she accompanies with a flapping of the ears. The 'mew' of this species can best be compared to the roar of the Tiger but pitched an octave higher and with only slightly less volume.

Some authors state that this species is aggressively anti-social but others have found the opposite to be true. It has also been postulated that in the wild the Black-footed Cat is monogamous, experience with captive animals casts doubt on this. This may be the practical application of the 'Harvard Law of Animal Behaviour' which states that 'under the most carefully controlled experimental conditions the animal will do as it damn well pleases'. This species is almost exclusively ground dwelling.

Breeding

Studies in South Africa indicate that while this species does breed throughout the year there is a strong peak of births in November and December. The female appears to be in oestrous for only one or two days during which time she is receptive to the male for only about ten hours. This pattern may be the consequence of the nature of the country in which the cat lives, small cats in the open for long periods would be very vulnerable to predators.

The kittens are usually said to be reared in burrows, this seems to be confirmed by one captive female who heaped sand around the entrance to a small sandstone den, on an occasion when she gave birth outside she refused to rear the kittens. To counter this suggestion, in the wild, very small kittens have been found under bushes.

Observation of captive births indicates a bias towards male kittens of 5:4.

Development of Young

At birth the eyes and ears are shut and the kittens seem unable to retract their claws. Their feet are pink and do not become black until they are about six weeks old. When the kittens are newborn it is possible to see that their colouring comes, not from a pigmented area of skin, but from pigments in the hairs themselves.

The eyes open at about eight or nine days old and by the fourteenth day the ears are open. The canines and incisors erupt at about eighteen days while the premolars appear at about twenty-six days of age. The permanent canines appear at about twenty-one weeks of age.

On the fourth day some individuals are able to sit and at two weeks they are able to walk and start indulging in play. They start leaving the nest between the third and fourth weeks, and at six weeks they are running with a bounding motion. When the kittens can run well they respond to danger by running away from their mother into any available cover, where they freeze until she gives them the 'all clear'.

The kittens are able to purr from birth, spitting and other vocalization are soon perfected by practice.

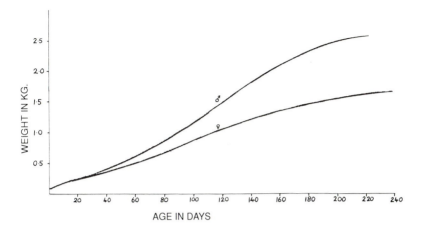

Average weight gain in Black-footed Cat Kittens

Status and Systematics

This species is fairly common and is apparently plentiful in some parts of its range. It is closely related to the Wild Cat, and there are generally reckoned to be two sub-species.

The International Species Indexing System numbers are as follows:

1412007001019	Black-footed Cat File Number	
1412007001019001	*Felis nigripes*	General Entry
1412007001019002	*Felis nigripes nigripes*	South West Africa
		South Africa
1412007001019003	*Felis nigripes thomasi*	East Cape Province

Chapter Eight

CHINESE DESERT CAT
Felis bieti Milne Edwards 1892

Vital Statistics

Length	head and body	70 - 85 cm.
	tail	29 - 35 cm.
Weight		approx. 5.5 kg.

Description

This little known species is larger than the Domestic Cat. The ground colour of the coat is yellowish grey with reddish tinges on the back. There are indistinct bands on the cheeks and transverse bands on the haunches. The tail has black rings and a black tip. There are long hairs scattered throughout the winter coat and hairy pads on the soles of the feet.

The skull is broad with large auditory vesicles, these, coupled with the presence of pencil tufts on the ears indicates that this cat does much of its hunting by sound.

Distribution

This cat is found in the border area of Eastern Tibet and Western China, in the provinces of Kansu and Szechwan.

Habitat and Habits

Within its range this species lives in steppe country and on mountains covered with shrubs and thin forests, it is known to live as high as 3,000 metres above sea level. There is one report of a Chinese Desert Cat biting a dog after having been chased by it.

Status and Systematics

It is not known how rare or plentiful this cat is but from the fact that only a few skins have ever been seen it must be presumed to be fairly scarce.

The International Species Indexing System numbers are:-

1412007001004	Chinese Desert Cat File Number	
1412007001004001	*Felis bieti*	General Entry
1412007001004002	*Felis bieti bieti*	Kansu, Szechwan

Chapter Nine

SERVAL
Leptailurus serval **Schreber 1776**

Vital Statistics

Length	head and body	70 - 90 cm.
	tail	36 - 45 cm.
Height at shoulder		40 - 65 cm.
Weight		14 - 18 kg.
Age at Maturity		approx. 18 months
Dental formula		$I \, {}^3/_3 \quad C \, {}^1/_1 \quad P \, {}^3/_2 \quad M \, {}^1/_1$
Chromosome count		38
Karyotype		1 (Robinson)
Longevity		approx. 19 years
Gestation period		70 - 77 days
Number of young		1 - 5
Weight at birth		approx. 250 g.
Young weaned		4 - 5 months

Description

The Serval is a medium sized elegant looking cat with very long legs, a relatively small head and very large ears. The ground colour of the coat is yellowish buff with the underparts pale, almost white. There are black spots on the body which merge into stripes on the neck and upper part of the back. The short tail has spots, which become rings towards the tip, whilst the tip itself is black. The backs of the ears are black with white centres and there are collar markings in the form of black stripes.

There are many variations in colouring and coat pattern including a small spotted form which is sometimes known as the 'Servaline'. Occasionally individuals are found with no spots at all, melanistic specimens are common in East Africa and are recorded elsewhere. The female normally has two pairs of teats.

Distribution

There is a remnant population in Algeria and Morocco, otherwise the Serval is found South of the Sahara with an extension of the range into Ethiopia. In the Republic of South Africa it is not found in the centre or South West, nor is it found in Southern Namibia.

Habitat

The Serval will live in almost any sort of country whether it is steppe, savannah, or scrubland; it is however more common in moist savannah. This cat may be found in tall reeds and grass but will always be close to a river or other source of water. It is also found on high mountain moorland.

Habits

The Serval is primarily a nocturnal animal though sometimes it may be seen hunting in the early morning or late afternoon. Most of its hunting takes place on the ground but it will occasionally leap up to knock down small low flying birds. The Serval locates its prey by sound then springs high in the air and pounces down on its quarry. Sometimes it will catch small animals such as rodents by digging them up; rodents are also snatched from clefts in rocks.

The prey includes rodents, hares, hyraxes, lizards, frogs and insects as well as small and young antelopes; they have even been seen taking fishes out of the water with their paws.

When chased the Serval will flee and will even climb trees to evade capture, although this is not part of the normal behaviour. They will also enter water and are capable of swimming well. In spite of its long legs it is not able to run as fast as the Cheetah, this is because in the Serval the metatarsals are lengthened, rather than the forearm, as in the Cheetah.

Servals hold a territory that is fairly extensive, that of the male may be as much as nineteen square kilometres and that of the female, seventeen square kilometres. While the territory of a male may overlap that of several females, the Serval is by nature a solitary animal.

Breeding

Servals are only seen together in pairs during courtship, it appears that the female only remains in oestrous for one day though oestrous may occur at any time of the year. From this it will be seen that in the wild the Serval does not have a fixed breeding season, though there seems to be a peak in the late summer.

The den where the female gives birth may be the abandoned burrow of a boar, an Aardvark, or a porcupine, alternatively it may be in a large grass mound. In captivity the female remains fertile up to the age of fourteen years.

Development of Young

When born the kittens are blind and their eyes do not open until they are about nine days old. When they are eleven days old they have almost doubled their birth weight. From then until they are about nine months old they gain about ten grams per day. They will start to eat solid food at about eleven weeks and are entirely weaned at four to five months. They start to gain their permanent teeth at about six and a half months.

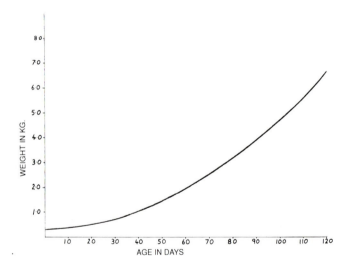

Average weight gain in Serval Kittens

Status and Systematics

The Serval has few enemies apart from man and the Leopard, it is hunted for its coat and is becoming rare in some parts of its range. In some places it has now been given official protection and this may help it to recover.

Whilst previously classified with the Wild Cats the Serval is now placed on its own in the Genus *Leptailurus*. There are considered to be fourteen sub-species.

The International Species Indexing System numbers are as follows:-

1412007001025	Serval File Number	
1412007001025001	*Leptailurus serval*	General Entry
1412007001025002	*Leptailurus serval serval*	Cape Province
1412007001025003	*Leptailurus serval beirae*	Mozambique
1412007001025004	*Leptailurus serval brachyura*	Sierra Leone to Ethiopia
1412007001025005	*Leptailurus serval constantina*	Algeria
1412007001025006	*Leptailurus serval hamiltoni*	East Transvaal
1412007001025007	*Leptailurus serval hindeio*	Tanzania
1412007001025008	*Leptailurus serval ingridi*	Zimbabwe, Botswana, South West Africa
1412007001025009	*Leptailurus serval kempi*	Uganda
1412007001025010	*Leptailurus serval kivuensis*	Congo, Angola
1412007001025011	*Leptailurus serval lipostica*	North Angola
1412007001025012	*Leptailurus serval lonnbergi*	South West Angola
1412007001025013	*Leptailurus serval mababiensis*	North Botswana
1412007001025014	*Leptailurus serval robertsi*	West Transvaal
1412007001025015	*Leptailurus serval togoensis*	Dahomey and Togo

Chapter Ten

CARACAL
Caracal caracal Schreber 1776

Vital Statistics

Length	head and body	60 - 75 cm.
	tail	22 - 30 cm.
Height at Shoulder		40 - 50 cm.
Weight		male up to 17 kg.
		female up to 14 kg.
Age at maturity		approx. 2 years
Dental formula		$I^3/_3 \quad C^1/_1 \quad P^2/_2 \quad M^1/_1$
Chromosome count		38
Karyotype		1 (Robinson)
Longevity		17 years
Gestation period		approx. 71 days
Number of young		1 - 6
Young weaned		approx. 10 weeks

Description

A medium sized cat which is nevertheless smaller than the Lynx. The ground colour of the coat varies from a reddish fawn to a russet brown which often has a metallic sheen to it. The coat is uniformly short and thick with a short tail and very long pencil tufts on the ears which are themselves long and are black on the back, the colour of the coat is paler, and occasionally white on the undersides. There are white rings around the eyes and a black line runs from the eyes to the nose. Young kittens are exact duplicates of their parents but with the black and white markings on the face standing out more boldly.

Melanistic individuals have been recorded in the wild but only one has been born in captivity.

The female has two pairs of teats.

Distribution

This species is found from central India through Afghanistan northwards into Turkmenistan, westwards into Iran and Arabia as far as the Mediterranean including Asia Minor. From

Israel the range goes southward to Sinai and South West through the whole of Africa except the equatorial rainforest, the Sahara desert and parts of the Republic of South Africa.

Habitat

Within this range the species inhabits many different types of country, typically it prefers desert fringes together with savannah, broken stony ground, scrub and mountain ranges. It is absent from truly arid desert and from dense forest although there is a report of one being sighted in the forests on Mount Marsabit.

Habits

Except during courtship and mating the Caracal is a solitary animal. It is primarily nocturnal although it is by no means unusual to see it about in daylight. It is little studied though and it may be more diurnal than we suspect. The species is mainly terrestrial but has been known to climb in order to escape capture, to catch prey, or to cache a kill. It is a quick and accurate jumper.

What little is known of this species indicates that it obtains most of its fluid requirements from its prey, so that it does not need to drink for several days. The range of animals preyed upon by the Caracal is extremely wide. Mammalian prey consists of antelopes such as duiker, and the young of much larger mammals, including a Greater Kudu fawn have been recorded. Baboons, Vervet Monkeys, rodents and a large mongoose have also been recorded. Avian prey may be caught on the ground, in the trees or knocked down whilst flying low. This last method is of course indicative of diurnal behaviour. The birds recorded as Caracal prey range from pigeons through to peafowl and cranes.

There are also records of Tawny Martial Eagles being taken, these must surely have been taken in trees whilst roosting. Lizards, cobra and domestic animals also form part of the prey on occasions.

The calls of the Caracal include a bird like chirruping which is often used between youngsters at play and by females in oestrous.

Breeding

There does not appear to be a fixed breeding season although local factors encourage a peak in July and August in South Africa and September to December in Zimbabwe. The den is usually the abandoned burrow of an Aardvark or a Porcupine. Alternative locations may be a hollow tree base, a hollow bush, or even a rock crevice. The male plays no part in the upbringing of the kittens.

Development of Young

When born the kittens are exact replicas of the parents with their eyes shut and their ears folded. The eyes open around the ninth or tenth day but the ears do not become erect until around the thirtieth day. In captivity they are observed to leave the nest at about three weeks old and straight away they begin playing chase, they frequently start eating solid food at about six weeks. Suckling ends at about ten weeks old. When they are about three months old they can defend themselves in an aggressive manner, it appears that they remain with their mother for about a year.

They become sexually mature at about twenty one months to two years, although in captivity at least one individual conceived at eighteen months.

Status and Systematics

In Asia the Caracal is listed as being 'at risk', the African Caracal is locally common, and rare elsewhere.

There are generally reckoned to be nine sub-species.

The International Species Indexing System numbers are as follows:-

1412007001005	Caracal File Number	
1412007001005001	*Caracal caracal*	General Entry
1412007001005002	*Caracal caracal caracal*	Sudan - Cape Province
1412007001005003	*Caracal caracal algira*	North Africa
1412007001005004	*Caracal caracal damarensis*	Damaraland, South West Africa
1412007001005005	*Caracal caracal limpopoensis*	North Transvaal, Botswana

1412007001005006	*Caracal caracal lucani*	Gabon
1412007001005007	*Caracal caracal michaelis*	Turkmenia
1412007001005008	*Caracal caracal nubicus*	Sudan, Ethiopia
1412007001005009	*Caracal caracal poecilictis*	Niger, Nigeria
1412007001005010	*Caracal caracal schmitzi*	Central India to Arabia

CHAPTER ELEVEN

LYNX
Felis lynx Linnaeus 1758

Vital Statistics

Length	head and body	80 - 130 cm.
	tail	11 - 24.5 cm.
Height at shoulder		60 - 75 cm.
Weight		18 - 35 kg.
Age of maturity		male 33 months
		female 21 months
Dental formula		$I\,^3/_3 \quad C\,^1/_1 \quad P\,^2/_2 \quad M\,^1/_1$
Chromosome count		38
Karyotype		1 (Robinson)
Longevity		24 years
Gestation period		63 - 68 days
Number of young		1 - 5
Weight at birth		approx. 260 g.

Description

The Lynx is a medium sized cat with fairly long fur which grows longer in winter. The ground colour of the coat is usually grey although it may vary from grey to yellowish-brown. Some individuals have plain coats and some have black spots on the back, flanks and legs, in general Lynx from central and southern Europe are more distinctly spotted than others; in Scandinavia both forms are found side by side. The paws are well covered with fur to protect the pads from damp and snow, this long fur gives a 'snow-shoe' effect. Both sexes have long cheek beards and the ears are large, well pointed with long tufts on the tips and black backs. The tip of the tail is black both above and below.

Distribution

The Lynx is found in Europe, Asia and North America. In Europe it is found in Germany and thence eastwards and northwards into Scandinavia. Efforts at re-introduction are currently being made in France, Italy and Switzerland. In Asia it is found in all the sub-Arctic areas with the exception of the hot lands of Central and southern India and Thailand, it is also absent from Indo-China. In North America it is found throughout Canada South of the tree line and extending into the United States as far South as Pennsylvania and New York State, in the West it is found down into Colorado and the Sierra Nevada, in the mid-West it is certainly found in Minnesota and may occur further South.

Habitat

Within its range the Lynx frequents woodland, preferably dense forest with thick undergrowth and windfalls. Over most of its range it is also found in dense shrubland. In Mongolia the Lynx lives in terrain where rocky outcrops alternate with shrubs, in the Altai it is not found above the tree line (about 1,800 metres). The most inhospitable habitat that it frequents is the bleak treeless uplands of Ladak. In America it keeps mostly to mountainous forests of the temperate zones sometimes extending further South since it is recorded from northern California.

Habits

The Lynx is basically solitary and its hunting behaviour is very largely nocturnal. An adult Lynx holds a territory which varies in size according to the type of country where it lives, this territory may be as little as 1,000 hectares or as much as 10,000 hectares. There are also outlying areas on the fringes of the territories which they visit occasionally and share with other Lynx. Territories are marked by spraying with urine and by scratching tree trunks; faeces are normally buried although on the boundaries of a territory they may be left exposed as marks. Lynx also defecate outside their own territory but the significance of this is not known. Females do not appear to use scratching trees when marking their territory. When conditions are not favourable Lynx may migrate over long distances, one female was recorded as moving 483 kilometres in ten weeks.

Lynx normally hunt alone but there is one report of two Lynx co-operating in a hunt. They are chiefly active during the early morning and late afternoon; at night and during the greater part of the day they sleep in a den away from wind and weather. Preferred sites are hollow trees, rock crevices and occasionally dense scrub.

Prey is located by sight and sound with the Lynx often lying in wait on a hillock or tree bough. The almost legendary eyesight of a Lynx can detect a mouse moving at 75 metres and a Roe Deer at 600 metres. Having located the prey the Lynx stalks the animal and, at the final moment pounces, deer are usually killed by biting the neck or the throat. The range of prey, in size, is from deer and Wild Boar down to mice, many different birds are eaten with the Lynx frequently springing into the air to bring them down. Often with large prey the Lynx does not return to consume a second meal and thus does the scavengers a favour. In North America the Lynx is so dependant on the Varying Hare *(Lepus americanus)* for its food that the Lynx population fluctuates in response to alterations in the numbers of Hares. A drop in the Lynx population occurring three to four years after a drop in the number of Hares. The length of the full cycle being about nine and a half years. The main enemies of the Lynx are the Leopard, Puma, and Man.

In the Altai mountains the proportions of the prey are:-

Roe Deer *(Capreolus capreolus)*	59%
Maral *(Cervus elaphus)*	14%
Musk Deer *(Moschus sps.)*	9%
Blue Hares *(Lepus timidus)*	7%
Carrion	5%
Capercaillie *(Tetrao urogallus)*	2%
Domestic Sheep *(Ovis aries)*	4%

In Poland the proportions are:-

Deer	7%
Hares	50%
Game Birds	15%
Mice and other rodents	10%
Other mammals	5%
Other prey	2%

In the Carpathians the Lynx has had a serious effect on the Roe Deer and the proportions are:-

Roe Deer *(Capreolus capreolus)*	14%
Wild Boar *(Sus scrofa)*	20%
Hare *(Lepus sps.)*	20%
Birds	16%
Mice	15%
Other Mammals	12%

In Sweden the diet is:-

Reindeer *(Rangifer tarandus)*	62%
Other deer	28%
Grouse *(Lyrurus tetrix)*	5%
Foxes, hares and rodents	5%

Breeding

Lynx have a fixed breeding season with mating taking place in February and March. During the breeding season females often leave their territories in order to find a mate, returning to their home range after mating. There are various accounts of mating behaviour, one report states that dominant males occupy a rutting stand and are visited by females who reportedly compete for his attentions. Other males do not approach nearer than a few kilometres from where they court females who have been chased away.

Other accounts are of several males courting one female with fierce fights breaking out over possession of the female. It is possible that both accounts may be true and be dependant on the balance of the local population. It is at this time of the year that the Lynx is at its most vocal, with both males and females indulging in very loud caterwauling.

The female gives birth in a den which may be in any safe secluded spot, examples which have been found are, natural caves, badger sets, overhanging rocks, under tree roots and even old stork nests. The male normally takes no part in rearing the kittens.

The composition of the maternal milk is:-

Water	81.5%
Fat	6.2%
Protein	10.2%
Carbohydrates	4.5%
Ash	0.75%

Development of Young

The kittens when born are fully furred and are usually blind. Their eyes open between eight and seventeen days of age. After one month they will take an interest in solid food, but will continue to suckle for as long as five months. At around three weeks the kittens are only just able to crawl and at about five weeks will begin to leave the den, development is very rapid and at about nine weeks the kittens can climb with great agility. By the time that they are fourteen weeks old they have gained their teeth and are engaged in combat over food and precedence.

It would appear that they leave their mother when she is ready to be mated in the next year. Males usually become mature at about thirty-three months old, and females at about twenty-one months. In captivity they will mature earlier.

Status and Systematics

In America the Lynx is fairly common and is holding its numbers, in Europe the species is fairly rare although it is slowly increasing its population and is also being re-introduced into its former haunts. In 1983 Lynx from a collection in England were introduced into southern France, and as far as can be ascertained these are adapting successfully. In Asia the Lynx is trapped for its fur but, although little is known about its numbers, it is thought to be safe from extinction.

There are usually considered to be nine sub-species. Some authorities include the Spanish Lynx in this species.

The International Species Indexing System Numbers are as follows:-

1412007001015	Lynx File Number	
1412007001015001	*Felis lynx*	General Entry
1412007001015002	*Felis lynx lynx*	Europe - Yenesei, Siberia
1412007001015003	*Felis lynx canadensis*	Canada - North U.S.A.
1412007001015004	*Felis lynx dinniki*	North Caucasus, Iraq
1412007001015005	*Felis lynx kozlowi*	Irkutsk
1412007001015006	*Felis lynx isabellina*	Kashmir, Central Russia Asia and Mongolia
1412007001015007	*Felis lynx sardiniae*	Sardinia
1412007001015008	*Felis lynx stroganovi*	Russia
1412007001015009	*Felis lynx subsolanus*	Newfoundland
1412007001015010	*Felis lynx wrangelli*	Siberia (East of Yenesei)

Chapter Twelve

SPANISH LYNX
Felis pardina Linnaeus 1758

Vital Statistics

Length	head and body	85 - 110 cm.
	tail	12.5 - 13 cm.
Height at Shoulder		60 - 70 cm.
Weight		15 - 25 kg.
Age at maturity		male 33 months
		female 21 months
Dental Formula		$I\,^3/_3 \quad C\,^1/_1 \quad P\,^2/_2 \quad M\,^1/_1$
Chromosome Count		38
Karyotype		1 (Robinson)
Gestation period		63 - 68 days
Number of young		1 - 5
Weight at birth		200 - 250 g.
Age Weaned		5 months.

Description

A medium sized cat slightly smaller than the northern Lynx, the cheek-beards and ear tufts are longer than those of the northern Lynx. The coat is pale coloured and the spots are clearly defined while the fur is short. The large round paws grow thick tufts of hair in winter, this gives a snow-shoe effect.

Distribution

The mountains of Spain and Portugal and also the less frequented coastal regions such as the Cota Donana. It may also be present in the Carpathian mountains and the Balkan peninsula, although there is great doubt about the systematics of the species, and this distribution should be considered in conjunction with that of the Lynx.

Habitat and Habits

This cat is found principally in woodlands, though it may also live in areas of open scrubland providing that there is sufficient cover. Most individuals are confined to mountainous country.

Basically this cat is nocturnal and terrestrial though it may be occasionally seen in daylight. It is almost certainly a solitary animal with male and female only coming together at breeding time. The size of the territory varies from four to ten square kilometres. It is said to be a good jumper and a good swimmer.

Prey consists of rabbits, hares, squirrels, deer and sheep, occasionally birds, fish and insects are also eaten. The Lynx locates its prey by sight and sound and attacks it by pouncing on it and killing it with its teeth, often by using a neck bite. When the prey is large the Lynx has been known to bury the excess and return to the site for another meal. There are reports of Lynx knocking Red-Legged Partridge *(Alectoris rufa)* down in flight.

Vocalizations appear to consist mainly of shrill spitting sounds, during courtship individuals have been heard to make a screeching miaow which sometimes changes to a deep bass sound.

Breeding

The Spanish Lynx probably mates in January and at this time may be found outside its normal territory, it appears that the males occupy special mating sites, and are then sought out by females. Master males will keep other males away and these then have to be content with less favourable sites.

Birth takes place in a secluded place.

Development of Young

The kittens are born blind and relatively helpless. Their eyes open after about two weeks and they start taking solid food at about five weeks. They are fully weaned at about five months old and become independent at the beginning of the next mating season. Kittens will reach full adulthood between two and three years of age.

Status and Systematics

The Spanish Lynx is regarded as an endangered animal and receives full protection.

The taxonomic position of the Spanish Lynx is a subject for much argument; some authorities believe it is a separate species, and some regard it as merely a sub-species of the Lynx.

The International Species Indexing System numbers are as follows:-

1412007001021	Spanish Lynx File Number	
1412007001021001	*Felis pardina*	Iberian Peninsula

Chapter Thirteen

BOBCAT, BAY LYNX
Felis rufus Schreber 1777

Vital Statistics

Length	head and body	male 86 cm.
		female 80 cm.
	tail	male 15 cm.
		female 14 cm.
Height at shoulder		53 cm.
Weight		male 9.6 kg.
		female 6.7 kg.
		average, considerable variation occurs through range.
Dental formula		I $^3/_3$ C $^1/_1$ P $^2/_2$ M $^1/_1$
Chromosome count		38
Karyotype		1 (Robinson)
Longevity approx.		32 years
Gestation period		50 - 60 days
Number of young		1 - 6
Weight at birth		approx. 300 g.
Age weaned		3 - 5 months

Description

The Bobcat looks superficially like a small stocky Lynx, the tufts on the ears are smaller and the tip of the tail is black only on top. The fur varies in colour from shades of grey to shades of reddish brown with 'tabby like' markings on the face, forehead and chest. There may be black spots on the coat although many individuals are completely unspotted. The darkest and smallest individuals occur in the southern U.S.A. and Mexico whilst the largest and palest are found in Canada. The backs of the ears are black. Both albino and melanistic specimens have been recorded.

Distribution

The Bobcat is found in every State of the U.S.A. and is found as far South as southern Mexico. Bobcats are also found in the southern part of every Canadian Province.

Habitat

The Bobcat will live in almost any type of country with the exceptions that it will not live in treeless, shrubless plains, nor in thick rain forest. Generally in steep hilly country it prefers broken woodland or cane breaks. There are few records of it occurring at altitudes over 1,800 metres, and none at all above 3,700 metres.

Habits

The Bobcat is a shy and secretive animal, but it is, nevertheless more tolerant of man's presence than many cats. It will hunt by night close to human settlements and in areas where it feels safe it will do so by day.

Territory is marked by piles of droppings left at significant points, urine sprays on rocks and bushes near dens seem to be intended to keep other animals away. Bobcats also communicate with each other by using scrapes. The territories of males are too large to be defended, in some cases they may be up to 173 square kilometres, this leads to a situation where the territories of several males overlap. Female territories, are about 16 square kilometres and are much better defined. It is likely that cats whose ranges do overlap will space themselves out so that they do not meet; there is however a report of three Bobcats sharing the same rock pile for two weeks, each had a different entrance and hunting area. Whilst the species is basically terrestrial it will, if threatened, climb trees extremely well.

The voice of the Bobcat, when threatened, is a low whine which becomes a growl and finally a bark like cough which is so loud that it may startle even people used to hearing it. When contented the Bobcat may purr just like a Domestic Cat. The loudest vocalizations are emitted during courtship, when, according to observers, the hisses, screams and yowls are like those of the alley cat magnified many times.

The Bobcats preferred method of hunting is to stalk its prey, pounce onto its back and kill it with a neck bite, another method frequently observed is ambush alongside rabbit tracks. Bobcats have been known to bury uneaten prey in order to retrieve it later, more frequently though they will gorge themselves leaving any excess for scavengers.

The principal item of prey for Bobcats is the rabbit, in some areas these animals form over 60% of the diet; this means that a fall in rabbit numbers will result in a similar decline in the population of Bobcats. Other prey includes deer, rodents, poultry, raccoon, opossum and quail, other wild animals and some domestic livestock are also taken. The largest animal recorded as being killed by a Bobcat is a deer *(Odocoileus)* weighing 68 kg. At the other end of the scale they will eat invertebrates and vegetation.

The main enemies of the Bobcat are Man, Puma, Jaguar, and possibly Lynx; Wild boar and deer have been seen to attack Bobcat at various times.

Breeding

There are indications that the Bobcat can, at least in some areas, breed at any time of the year. In most areas however the breeding season is between February and June. It is probable that, as in other species, if the first litter is lost for any reason the female will come back into oestrous within about two weeks. It appears that males are sexually active at all times of the year.

The most commonly found den sites are under logs in thickets, the root hollows of windfall trees, and small rocky caves. Females will sometimes prepare the den with bedding of moss and leaves, in the wild females will only give birth every two years.

Development of Young

The kittens are born blind and gain their sight when between three and nine days old. They will continue to suckle from their mother until approximately two months old, when they start eating meat. Both the male and female bring food to the den.

The kittens first start to leave the den when about five weeks old and, when they are about five months old the female will take them on hunting forays to teach them the skills of hunting. Some individuals become partially independent at about seven months, keeping only a sporadic contact with their mother. Some time after they are nine months old the young become independent and then wander far and wide in search of a place to live.

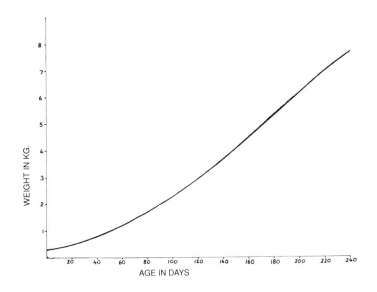

Weight gain in Bobcat Kittens

Status and Systematics

Over much of its range the Bobcat is holding its numbers, the areas where it is most in danger are those where it is being pushed aside by urban development and by dams for hydro-electric and irrigation schemes.

There are usually considered to be twelve sub-species.

The International Species Indexing System Numbers are as follows:-

1412007001024	Bobcat File Number	
1412007001024001	*Felis Rufus*	General Entry
1412007001024002	*Felis rufus rufus*	North Dakota, East Oklahoma, East Coast
1412007001024003	*Felis rufus baileyi*	South East California, Durango, West Kansas
1412007001024004	*Felis rufus californicus*	California
1412007001024005	*Felis rufus escuinapae*	Central Mexico

1412007001024006	*Felis rufus fasciatus*	South British Columbia - North West California.
1412007001024007	*Felis rufus floridianus*	East Louisiana, East Arkansas, South Carolina Florida
1412007001024008	*Felis rufus gigas*	Maine borders
1412007001024009	*Felis rufus pallescens*	British Columbia Nevada - Colorado
1412007001024010	*Felis rufus peninsularis*	Baja, California
1412007001024011	*Felis rufus superiorensis*	Minnesota, North Wisconsin, Michigan, South Ontario
1412007001024012	*Felis rufus texensis*	Texas - North East Mexico
1412007001024013	*Felis rufus uinta*	North East Washington North Dakota, North Nevada, North Mexico

Chapter Fourteen

PALLAS'S CAT, MANUL
Otocolobus manul Pallas 1776

Vital Statistics

Length	head and body	50 - 65 cm.
	tail	21 - 31 cm.
Weight		3 - 5.5 kg.
Dental Formula		$I^3/_3$ $C^1/_1$ $P^2/_2$ $M^1/_1$
Longevity		11 years 6 months
Gestation Period		60 - 65 days
Number of young		4 - 6
Weight at birth		70 - 100 g.

Description

The Pallas's Cat is about the size of a Domestic Cat, with a large body carried on short legs. The head is short and broad with the ears set low down, the eyes are large, round and forward looking like those of an owl, The coat, the fur of which is very long, has a ground colour varying from light grey to buff and russet, the tips of the hairs are white giving a frosted appearance to the coat. Dark stripes run across the cheeks and the tail has dark rings around it.

The kittens have a thick woolly coat which lacks the frosted appearance of the adults.

Distribution and Habitat

This species lives on the eastern shores of the Caspian Sea, in Afghanistan, Ladak, Mongolia, Western China and neighbouring parts of southern Russia.

The sort of country that Pallas's Cat prefers is open terrain such as steppe, desert and treeless rocky mountain sides. There are reports of it being seen more than 4,000 metres above sea level.

Habits

Pallas's Cat is exclusively terrestrial and when at home on rocky mountain sides it is an extremely good climber. Most of its hunting is done by night although it may occasionally be seen during the day. This cat is by nature solitary and secretive and likes to make its den in the burrow of another animal or else in a small cleft in the rocks. The prey consists of pikas, rodents, insectivores and birds, the low set ears enable this cat to conceal itself better to ambush in open country whilst maintaining a constant listening watch for possible prey. There is also a well developed nictitating membrane which may be an adaptation to protect the eyes in the extreme cold and wind of the high places in which it lives.

In captivity individuals vary in their reactions, some of them showing irritation by a hiss and others by a shrill sound through closed lips. This cat also makes a noise which is something between a small dog barking and an owl screeching, those who have heard it believe that it is the mating call of this cat.

Breeding

Very little is known about the breeding habits of this species. It is recorded that in Mongolia and Turkestan births take place in April and May, and that there can be as many as six kittens. There is said to be a high mortality rate in the first year.

In captive bred animals at birth the kittens weigh around 70 - 100 g. This increases to about 500 g. at seven weeks, from then on the weight increases rapidly so that at ten weeks they weigh 750 - 850 g. By the time that they are eight months old they have reached their full adult size and weight.

The weight gain shown in the graph refers to one kitten.

Status and Systematics

Pallas's Cat occurs in small pockets throughout its range and it is considered to be rare.

Due to its strange characteristics it is placed by itself in the Genus *Otocolobus*. There are generally considered to be three sub-species.

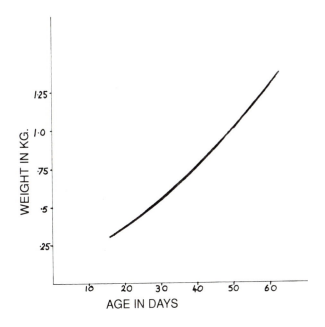

Weight gain recorded in a Pallas Cat Kitten

The International Species Indexing System numbers are as follows:-

1412007001016	Pallas's Cat File Number	
1412007001016001	*Otocolobus manul*	General Entry
1412007001016002	*Otocolobus manul manul*	Mongolia and West China
1412007001016003	*Otocolobus manul ferruginea*	Turkestan, Iran and Afghanistan
1412007001016004	*Otocolobus manul nigripecta*	Tibet and Nepal

51

Chapter Fifteen

LEOPARD CAT
Prionailurus bengalensis Kerr 1792

Vital Statistics

Length	head and body	36 - 60 cm.
	tail	30 - 40 cm.
Weight		3 - 4 kg.
Age at maturity		approx. 18 months
Dental formula		$I\,{}^3/_3$ $C\,{}^1/_1$ $P\,{}^3/_2$ $M\,{}^1/_1$
Chromosome count		38
Karyotype		2 (Robinson)
Longevity		13 years 6 months
Gestation period		63 - 68 days
Number of young		1 - 4
Weight at birth		75 - 95 g.
Age weaned		approx 10 weeks

Description

A delicate little cat about the same size as the Domestic Cat, individuals found in the North of the range are usually larger, and those from the island races, in the South, smaller. The ground colour of the coat varies from rufous through shades of ochre to greyish, the underparts are white and the eyes are lined with white next to the nose and cheeks. Black bands run over the skull to form rows of elongated spots on the back of the neck, there are also black lines on the throat. There are black spots on the coat which, in the more northerly sub-species, become rosettes. The tail has black spots which form rings towards the tip, the tip is always black. The backs of the ears are black with white centres.

Distribution

The Leopard Cat is quite widespread in eastern Asia, it occurs in the Amur region of Siberia, throughout China, Tibet, Indo-China, Indonesia (except the Celebes and Irian), Malaysia, Burma and Thailand. It is also found in Central and Northern India and some of the Philippine Islands. It is now known to occur also on the Japanese Island of Tsushima.

Habitat

Within its range the Leopard Cat is found wherever there is sufficient cover in the form of bush and forest. Since it is highly dependant on water it avoids the more arid regions. It prefers relatively low country and it is never found above 3,000 metres.

Habits

The Leopard Cat is for most of the year a solitary animal that does most of its hunting at dusk and by night. It is however not unusual to see this cat about in daylight when it may be observed hunting for mice in the long grass. The Leopard Cat is a superb climber and is usually regarded as being semi-arboreal, however most of the animals that form its prey are ground dwelling, this, along with the evidence of trip wire photographs taken at night suggests that it may be very largely terrestrial. The den is made in a hollow tree, under a rocky overhang or under the roots of a tree, frequently the site chosen is near a village. The Leopard Cat is a good swimmer and is never found far from water, adults urinate and defecate in water whilst juveniles bury their faeces.

Their prey consists of a wide range of species, it includes the young of Roe Deer, (*Capreolus capreolus*), Musk Deer (*Moschus sps.*), Muntjac (*Muntiacus sps.*), hares, squirrels, rabbits, rats, mice and even bats. In Siberia it will eat fish and reptiles. Many game birds, jungle fowl and domestic chickens are also eaten. The prey is caught by stalking and then killed with a nape bite. In captivity juveniles have been seen eating grass and it is possible that they do so in the wild as well.

Breeding

The only time that Leopard Cats congregate is when they come together to breed, at this time several males may chase one female who is in season. There does not appear to be a fixed breeding season since kittens have been seen in the wild at all times of the year, in captivity also births take place throughout the year. It does appear that in Siberia births are concentrated at the end of May, which is what might be expected from the climate. Observations in captivity indicate that the female is in oestrous from between five and nine days and that the gestation period is between sixty and seventy days. In captivity males have been seen to assist in the raising of the kittens.

Development of Young

The kittens are born blind and they gain their sight at about ten days of age. When they are about two weeks old they start attempting to clean themselves and when three weeks old they start to play and to sharpen their claws, shortly after this they begin to eat solid meat.

They start to leave the den for the first time at about four weeks and from then on their development is rapid. Milk teeth are lost at about six months but they will not be mature until about eighteen months.

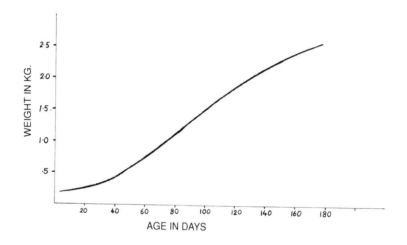

Average weight gain in Leopard Cat Kittens

Status and Systematics

In many parts of its range the Leopard Cat is endangered because it is killed for its coat; in some parts of its range however it is believed to be safe.

The systematics of this cat have caused endless confusion among taxonomists, both because of its wide range, and because of its variable coloration. It is now generally assigned to the Genus *Prionailurus* and is believed by some authorities to have ten subspecies.

The International Species Indexing System numbers are as follows:-

1412007001003	Leopard Cat File Number	
1412007001003001	*Prionailurus bengalensis*	General Entry
1412007001003002	*Prionailurus bengalensis bengalensis*	India- Indochina, Yunan
1412007001003003	*Prionailurus bengalensis borneoensis*	Borneo
1412007001003004	*Prionailurus bengalensis chinensis*	China and Taiwan
1412007001003005	*Prionailurus bengalensis euptailura*	East Siberia
1412007001003006	*Prionailurus bengalensis horsfieldi*	Kashmir - Sikkim
1412007001003007	*Prionailurus bengalensis manchurica*	Manchuria, Tsushima Island
1412007001003008	*Prionailurus bengalensis trevelyani*	North Kashmir, South Baluchistan
1412007001003009	*Prionailurus bengalensis javaensis*	Java
1412007001003010	*Prionailurus bengalensis minutus*	Philippines
1412007001003011	*Prionailurus bengalensis sumatranus*	Sumatra

Chapter Sixteen

RUSTY-SPOTTED CAT
Prionailurus rubiginosus Geoffroy 1834

Vital Statistics

Length	head and body	35 - 48 cm.
	tail	15 - 25 cm.
Weight		1 - 2 kg.

Description

A small cat with rounded ears and short, soft fur. The ground colour of the coat is greyish brown with a rufous tinge, the undersides are much lighter in colour. Dark stripes run over the forehead, these are bounded by two white stripes which extend down the side of the nose. The back and sides have rusty brown blotches arranged in lines, these blotches become paler towards the tail. The tail may be either plain or have a few spots at the base. The Sri Lanka sub-species is more brightly rufous.

Distribution

The Rusty-Spotted Cat is found in southern India within the Central Provinces, the Carnatic and Gujerat, it is also found in the southern part of Sri Lanka.

Habitat and Habits

In India this cat is found in shrubland, dry grassland and open dry forest. In Sri Lanka on the other hand it is found in the humid jungles of the mountain regions in the South of the Island.

The Rusty-Spotted Cat does most of its hunting by night and is reportedly very agile. It is known that it marks its territory by spraying and defecating at regular posts. The prey consists of small mammals, birds and lizards, the method of hunting is not known, neither is the courtship behaviour. In India the kittens are born in the Spring.

Status and Systematics

Because of the difficulties of observing this cat nothing is known about its present numbers, the assumption is that it is rare.

There are just two sub-species.

The International Species Indexing System Numbers are as follows:-

1412007001023	Rusty-Spotted Cat File Number	
1412007001023001	*Prionailurus rubiginosus*	General Entry
1412007001023002	*Prionailurus rubiginosus rubiginosus*	Southern India
1412007001023003	*Prionailurus rubiginosus phillipsi*	Southern Sri Lanka

Chapter Seventeen

FISHING CAT
Prionailurus viverrinus Bennett 1833

Vital Statistics

Length	head and body	75 - 86 cm.
	tail	25.5 - 33 cm.
Height at shoulder		38 - 40.6 cm.
Weight		7.7 - 14 kg.
Dental formula		$I \frac{3}{3} \quad C \frac{1}{1} \quad P \frac{3}{2} \quad M \frac{1}{1}$
Chromosome count		38
Karyotype		2 (Robinson)
Longevity		up to 9 years
Gestation period		63 - 68 days
Number of young		1 - 4
Age weaned		7 - 8 weeks
Weight at birth		170 g.

Description

The Fishing Cat is larger than a Domestic Cat and in comparison gives the appearance of looking rather clumsy having a large broad head and a broad muzzle. The male is about a quarter larger than the female. The tail is fairly short and the fur is relatively short and coarse in texture. The ground colour of the coat is grizzled grey, sometimes tinged with brown, the markings consist of dark brown spots which are arranged in rows. There are dark lines running over the forehead. The ears are short and rounded with white spots on the backs. There are webs between the toes of the forefeet. The claw sheaths on the forefeet are not sufficiently large to contain the claws. The first upper premolar is very small.

Distribution and Habitat

This cat is widely distributed in South East Asia, and is found in India, Nepal, Burma, Thailand, Sri Lanka, Indochina, Indonesia, South China and Taiwan.

Within this range the Fishing Cat is mostly found in country where there is thick cover such as humid forests, mangrove swamps and marshy thickets. It is always found close to water. There are reports of it being seen as high as 1,500 metres above sea level.

Habits

Little is known of the behaviour of this animal in the wild. This is because it is a secretive cat and therefore difficult to observe. It is known that it will wade in shallow water to catch fish, and will even dive under water to catch them. It is certainly a fierce tempered cat and has been seen to rout a pack of dogs, there are even reports that it has carried off infants. It is difficult to know how much credence to give the latter report. There is a confirmed report that one newly caught individual broke through into the next door cage and killed a female Leopard that was twice its size. The Fishing Cat is certainly not afraid of approaching villages at night, although it is not exclusively a nocturnal animal.

The only vocalizations heard from this species have been during oestrous periods, the calls have been made by both male and female cats. These calls have been described as birdlike chirps.

The Fishing Cat preys on small mammals, birds, snakes and frogs as well as fishes, crustaceans and aquatic molluscs; it has also been known to attack larger prey such as cattle.

Breeding and Development of Young

Some authorities believe that the Fishing Cat breeds throughout the year with births rising to a peak both in April and October. In captivity it is reported that male and female will live in harmony together with their kittens but it is not known if this is so in the wild.

The kittens are born in a lair that may consist of beaten down reeds with tunnelled approaches. The kittens are born blind and their eyes open at about sixteen days. They start to leave the nest at about twenty-eight days. Meat is first eaten at about eight weeks and they reach their full adult size at about thirty-eight weeks.

Status and Systematics

The Fishing Cat is considered to be fairly rare, though this may be because of the difficulties of observation.

There is only one subspecies.

The International Species Indexing System Numbers are:-

1412007001029   Fishing Cat File Number
1412007001029001   *Prionailurus viverrinus viverrinus*

Chapter Eighteen

IRIOMOTE CAT
Pronailurus iriomotensis Imaizumi 1967

Vital Statistics

Length	head and body	approx. 50 cm.
	tail	approx. 23 cm.
Weight		approx. 5.5 kg.
Dental formula		$I\,{}^3/_3$ $C\,{}^1/_1$ $P\,{}^2/_2$ $M\,{}^1/_1$
Gestation period		estimated at 60 - 70 days
Number of young		recorded litters of 1 and 2

Description

The Iriomote Cat is about the same size as a Domestic Cat with an elongated body, a short tail and short legs. The ground colour of the coat is dark brown, dark lines go over the forehead to the neck ending at the shoulders, there are also lines from the corners of the eyes going round the cheeks. The backs of the ears are black with central white spots, there are rows of dark spots on the body and the tail, which is thick and bushy, has dark rings round it at the end and blackish spots on the upper side at the base.

The claws are not capable of being fully retracted and remain more or less visible throughout life. The bullae are very small, this may indicate that sound plays a lesser part in the life of this species.

Distribution and Habitat

This cat is confined to Iriomote Island. The type of country which it lives in consists of steep hillsides and gullies which are thickly wooded and are cut by many rivers.

Habits

The Iriomote Cat is mainly nocturnal and, so far as is known, terrestrial. It has been found to have a seasonal pattern of movement, in Spring, Summer, and Autumn it spends its time up in the mountains only coming down to the lower plateaux in Winter.

Due to its low slung build it is able to make use of tunnels left in the thick undergrowth by the passage of the small Ryukyu Wild Boar. This cat appears to have a territory of about two square kilometres. It marks its territory with urine at signposts and does not bury its faeces. Because of the seasonal pattern of movement it is not known what function marking territory performs. A reasonable speculation is that it forms a communicating function because this cat is solitary except when breeding.

Prey includes ducks, rodents, crabs and mud skippers, while the cat itself probably falls prey to poisonous snakes.

Breeding

The new-born young are smaller than those of the Leopard Cat and are similar in size to those of the Domestic Cat. A male and female kitten examined in 1962 proved to be partial albinos.

Status and Systematics

This species was only officially described in 1967 and since it has such a restricted distribution and is known to be low in numbers it must be considered as vulnerable. One cause for concern is that the natives of Iriomote island catch the cat for eating.

This cat shows a resemblance to the Leopard Cat but with many juvenile characteristics, because of this it is included in the Genus *Prionailurus,* some authorities however place it in a separate Genus *Mayailurus.*

The International Species Indexing System Numbers are as follows:

1412007001012 Iriomote Cat File Number
1412007001012001 *Prionailurus iriomotensis iriomotensis*

Chapter Nineteen

FLAT-HEADED CAT
Prionailurus planiceps Vigors and Horsfield 1827

Vital Statistics

Length	head and body	53 - 61 cm.
	tail	15 - 20 cm.
Weight		5 - 8 kg.
Longevity		up to 6 years

Description

The Flat-Headed Cat is a strange looking animal, the skull is broad and flat yet at the same time elongated with the nose forming a ridge. The short legs and short tail also contribute to the strange appearance. The coat is thick and while the back and sides are a uniform reddish brown the undersides are white, on the face two white stripes run from the side of the nose up over the forehead. The ears are small with black backs that have an ochre spot at the base.

The claws are not fully retractable and are visible the whole time, however they are held up clear of the ground. The first upper premolar has two roots and unlike those of other cats is sharp and powerful, also all the other teeth are pointed.

The female normally has four pairs of teats.

Distribution and Habitat

Confined to Malaya, Sumatra and Borneo, the Flat-headed Cat lives in low country on the floors of forests and is always found close to water, whether river or swamp. There is a report of it being seen up to 700 metres above sea level.

Habits

The Flat-Headed Cat is almost exclusively nocturnal and does a lot of its hunting in the water, on occasions it has been caught in fish traps. The attachment of this cat to the water is so strong that one young individual was seen to wash its food raccoon style. The bulk of its diet appears to be fishes and crustaceans although it has been described as being destructive to gardens.

Breeding

The only information available concerning its breeding is a single report of one young animal being found in January.

Status and Systematics

Its status is indeterminate.

Whilst this cat is usually included in the Genus *Prionailurus* some authorities assign it to a separate Genus *Ictailurus*.

The International Species Indexing System numbers are as follows:-

1412007001022	Flat-Headed Cat File Number
1412007001022001	*Prionailurus planiceps planiceps*

Chapter Twenty

AFRICAN GOLDEN CAT
Profelis aurata Temminck 1827

Vital Statistics

Length	head and body	65 - 90 cm.
	tail	24 - 40 cm.
Height at shoulder		approx. 50 cm.
Weight		13 - 18 kg.
Age at Maturity		approx. 18 months
Dental formula		$I \frac{3}{3}$ $C \frac{1}{1}$ $P \frac{3}{2}$ $M \frac{1}{1}$
Chromosome count		38
Karyotype		1 (Robinson)
Longevity		12 years 2 months
Gestation period		approx. 75 days
Number of young		1 - 2
Weight at birth		180 - 240 g.
Age weaned		approx. 14 weeks

Description

The African Golden Cat is a medium sized cat considerably bigger than a Domestic Cat. The ground colour of the coat is usually golden brown although some individuals are coloured between greyish black and greyish blue. The cheeks, undersides and insides of the legs are white, some animals have spots all over the body whilst on others the spots are confined to the belly and legs. The tail has a dark line on the upper side and there are dark markings round the backs of the ears. The legs are of medium length in proportion to the body whilst the tail is long. Melanistic specimens have been recorded on many occasions. The female normally has two pairs of teats.

Distribution

The Golden Cat is found across most of Central Africa from Senegal in the West to the Mau forest of Kenya in the East. The strongholds for the species are the rain forests of West Africa and the Congo basin.

Habitat and Habits

The high forests and the edge of the savannah are the typical habitats. It sometimes ranges high into the mountains, where it has been recorded as high as 3,600 metres above sea level.

The Golden Cat is mainly crepuscular, apart from the fact that it is a solitary cat the few things that are known about this species are uncorroborated. Golden Cats are reported to be very fierce, to spend much of the day in the trees, and to stalk some of their prey in the trees as well.

Prey is reported to consist of birds, tree hyraxes and small antelope up to the size of duiker. The den is built in crevices, hollow trees or under rocks and shrubs.

Breeding and Development of Young

Little is known of the breeding of this species in the wild, however it has bred in captivity and a few things are known about the development of the young.

The kittens open their eyes by about the end of the first week and by the time they are two weeks old they are able to clamber around on their legs. After about three weeks of age they are able to jump onto low ledges and by the time that they are six weeks old they are able to eat solid food. The change to permanent dentition starts at around fourteen weeks, and is completed over the course of about seven weeks.

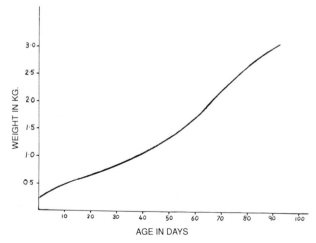

Average weight gain in African Golden Cat Kittens

Status and Systematics

Due to the elusiveness of this cat and the fact that the natives regard it as 'powerful medicine' it is difficult to gain a clear picture of its numbers. In the absence of any definitive information it must be regarded as rare.

Some authorities consider this cat to be con-specific with Asian Golden Cat. Those who regard it as a separate species cannot agree whether there are two or three sub-species.

The International Species Indexing System numbers are as follows:-

1412007001001	African Golden Cat File Number	
1412007001001001	*Profelis aurata*	General Entry
1412007001001002	*Profelis aurata aurata*	Congo - Uganda
1412007001001003	*Profelis aurata celidogaster*	West Africa
	Profelis aurata cottoni	Liberia - Cameroon

Chapter Twenty-one

TEMMINCK'S CAT, ASIATIC GOLDEN CAT
Profelis temmincki **Vigors and Horsfield 1828**

Vital Statistics

Length	head and body	73 - 105 cm.
	tail	48 - 56 cm.
Weight		6 - 16 kg.
Dental formula		$I\,^3/_3$ $C\,^1/_1$ $P\,^3/_2$ $M\,^1/_1$
Chromosome count		38
Karyotype		1 (Robinson)
Longevity		17 years 8 months
Gestation period		approx. 75 days
Number of young		1 - 3
Weight at birth		approx. 250 g.

Description

Temminck's Cat is a medium sized cat approximately the same size as the African Golden Cat. The ground colour of the coat varies greatly from grey through foxy-red to golden brown. Golden brown individuals have an almost metallic sheen to their coats. Normally there are no markings on the coat, a few specimens have some spots on the belly and in China there is a spotted sub-species which greatly resembles a large Leopard Cat. The backs of the ears are black with grizzled centres, the tail is white underneath for the third towards the tip. The face is the only part of the body with prominent markings which consist of white lines which run from above the eyes to the crown of the head. Melanistic specimens have been recorded on several occasions. The female normally has two pairs of teats.

Distribution

This species is confined to South East Asia, the area where it dwells comprises, Nepal, Sikkim, Assam, Tibet, Yunnan, Szechwan, thence East to Fu-kien and North to Kansu. The range continues South into Indochina, the Malaysian peninsula and Sumatra.

Habitat and Habits

Temminck's Cat inhabits dense forest, although it has been seen in sparse woods and rocky terrain.

The habits of this cat are little known, it isn't even certain whether it is nocturnal or diurnal. Some native tribesmen say that it never climbs trees, yet several specimens have been caught up trees. The author has heard a report that indicates that it is solitary and nocturnal. What is not known is what size the home range occupied by each individual is.

The range of prey taken by this cat is known to include birds, hares, muntjacs, and hog deer, domestic sheep, goats, and poultry have also been eaten by this cat.

Breeding and Development of Young

It is not known if Temminck's Cat has a fixed breeding season, although two births have been recorded in the Spring. After a captive birth the male was observed to tolerate the kittens and even participate in their upbringing. The female has been recorded as giving birth in a hollow tree and has up to three kittens.

Sight is gained by about ten days old and the milk incisors by about two weeks.

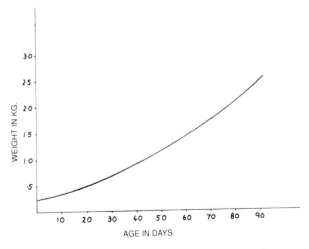

Average weight gain in Temmincks Cat Kittens

Status and Systematics

The exact status of this species is a matter for conjecture, however since there is a demand for its fur it is considered to be endangered.

Some authorities believe this cat to be con-specific with the African Golden Cat, but it is more usual to treat it as a separate species.

Most sources say that there are three sub-species.

The International Species Indexing System Numbers are as follows:-

1412007001027	Temminck's Cat File Number	
1412007001027001	*Profelis temmincki*	General Entry
1412007001027002	*Profelis temmincki temmincki*	Nepal - Malaya Indochina
1412007001027003	*Profelis temmincki dominicanorum*	South China
1412007001027004	*Profelis temmincki tristis*	Tibet, North Burma

Chapter Twenty-two

BAY CAT, BORNEAN RED CAT
Profelis badia Gray 1874

Vital Statistics

Length	head and body	50 - 60 cm.
	tail	35 - 40 cm.
Weight		2 - 3 kg.
Dental formula		$I^3/_3$ $C^1/_1$ $P^3/_2$ $M^1/_1$

Description

The Bay Cat resembles a small edition of the Temminck's Cat. The coat is golden brown on the back shading to pale chestnut on the belly, occasionally spots may be seen on the underparts and limbs. Faint stripes can be made out on the forehead and cheeks, the ears have blackish brown backs and are of normal size. The Bay Cat has a short rounded head and the first upper premolar is very small with only one root.

Distribution and Habitat

The Bay Cat, as its alternative name suggests, is only found in Borneo. Some reports state that it is only found in dense jungles while others say that it has a preference for rocky limestone areas on the edge of jungles. It is said to roam up to 900 metres above sea level.

Habits

Almost nothing is known about this species, it has a reputation for ferocity and is said to be such an adept climber that it can catch monkeys. It is known to eat carrion and catch small mammals.

If, as is suspected, it is related to the Temminck's Cat this would mean that it has a gestation of 75 - 85 days.

Status and Systematics

Its status is probably rare.

It is now the practice to classify the Bay Cat with the Golden Cats in the Genus *Profelis*. So far as is known there is only the one sub-species, the nominate one.

The International Species Indexing System numbers are as follows:-

1412007001002	Bay Cat File Number	
1412007001002001	*Profelis badia*	Borneo

Chapter Twenty-three

JAGUARUNDI
Herpailurus yagouarondi Geoffroy 1803

Vital Statistics

Length	head and body	55 - 77 cm.
	tail	33 - 60 cm.
Height at shoulder		25 - 35 cm.
Weight		4.5 - 9 kg.
Age at maturity		2 - 3 years
Dental formula		$I^3/_3$ $C^1/_1$ $P^3/_2$ $M^1/_1$
Chromosome count		38
Karyotype		3 (Robinson)
Longevity		up to 12 years
Gestation period		70 - 75 days
Number of young		1 - 4

Description

This cat has a thin face with a head almost like that of an otter. The ears are very small and the legs are very short, the tail is usually long, although there is considerable variation. The colour of the coat is uniform all over the body varying from black to light grey with brown and foxy red individuals occurring frequently. Some authorities state that the young are spotted at birth but those new born young seen by the author have been charcoal grey with plain coats. The eyes contract to a small circle.

Distribution

The Jaguarundi is found from Arizona and southern Texas southwards to Peru and northwest Argentina, it is also found in Paraguay and southern Brazil.

Habitat

The Jaguarundi is a lowland animal which is usually found at the edge of forests and in scrubland. It is never found in open country and only rarely found in dense forest.

Habits

This cat although capable of climbing well spends most of its time on the ground, it is more diurnal than most cats. Its build enables it to slink through the undergrowth whilst hunting, it will enter the water readily and swims well. In Arizona and Mexico the Jaguarundi is said to be solitary, whilst in other parts of its range it appears to live in couples which apparently share a common territory with other couples. Experience at one zoo indicates that they will congregate readily, and forming such groups has on at least two occasions provided a stimulus for breeding.

The diet consists mostly of birds, but mammals such as rodents, rabbits and small deer are also eaten. It is often said that individuals will eat fruit such as grapes or bananas. The author has known eight separate individuals and has found that all of them will completely ignore fruit.

Breeding and Development of the Young

Jaguarundis do not appear to have a fixed breeding season, this is supported by kittens being found at most times of the year. In captivity mating has been seen to take place throughout the year though births did not always take place.

The female is thought to favour thickets and hollow trees for her den. The kittens are born blind but fully furred. They start to venture outside the nest at about twenty-eight days of age, and start eating solid food at about five weeks. Growth is fairly rapid at first but slows down later, nevertheless they are fully grown by the end of their second year.

Status and Systematics

Their status is indeterminate.

There is some argument about the place of the Jaguarundi amongst the cats, some class it with the Puma, and some with the Flat-headed Cat, some even class it with the Fossa (*Cryptoprocta ferox*) which is usually thought of as a member of the family Viverridae. Usually however it is put by itself in the Genus *Herpailurus*. There are usually said to be eight subspecies.

The International Species Indexing System numbers are as follows:-

1412007001031	Jaguarundi File Number	
1412007001031001	*Herpailurus yagouarondi*	General entry
1412007001031002	*Herpailurus yagouarondi yagouarondi*	East Venezuela - North East Brazil
1412007001031003	*Herpailurus yagouarondi ameghinoi*	West Argentina
1412007001031004	*Herpailurus yagouarondi cacomitli*	South Texas - Central Vera Cruz
1412007001031005	*Herpailurus yagouarondi eyra*	South Brazil, Paraguay, North Argentina
1412007001031006	*Herpailurus yagouarondi fossata*	Veracruz - Central Nicaragua
1412007001031007	*Herpailurus yagouarondi melantho*	Peru
1412007001031008	*Herpailurus yagouarondi panamensis*	Central Nicaragua - Ecuador
1412007001031009	*Herpailurus yagouarondi tolteca*	South Arizona - Central Guerro

Chapter Twenty-four

OCELOT
Leopardus pardalis Linnaeus 1758

Vital Statistics

Length	head and body	60 - 100 cm.
	tail	27 - 45 cm.
Height at shoulder		40 - 50 cm.
Weight		5 - 21 kg.
Age at maturity		approx. 2½ years
Dental formula		$I^3/_3 \quad C^1/_1 \quad P^3/_2 \quad M^1/_1$
Chromosome count		36
Karyotype		5 (Robinson)
Longevity		up to 20 years
Gestation period		77 - 82 days
Number of young		1 - 3
Weight at birth		175 - 280 g.
Age weaned		approx. 9 weeks

Description

The Ocelot is a medium sized cat considerably larger than the Domestic Cat, it has within its own species a great deal of variation both in size and general appearance. The ground colour of the coat varies from shades of yellow to shades of grey or reddish grey. The markings on the back and sides resemble elongated spots with black outlines and a paler centre, these spots sometimes are arranged into chains of blotches. There are black lines going from the inner corners of the eyes over the forehead to the back of the neck, the legs are marked with spots on the outside and bars on the inside, the tail is usually ringed. The ears which are rounded have black borders on the back with white centres. The underside of the body and the insides of the legs are white. The female normally has two pairs of teats.

Distribution

The Ocelot is found in both North and South America, the northern boundary of the range running through Arizona, Texas and New Mexico. From there it ranges South through Central America and most of South America as far South as Peru and northern Argentina, it is however absent from Chile.

Habitat

Ocelots are found in many types of country where there is sufficient cover, dense humid forest, mountain forest and thick bush such as chaparral are all frequented by these cats. They may also be found in marshy areas and reed beds along river banks, they only appear to shun open areas.

Habits

The Ocelot is thought to live in pairs which occupy a well defined territory, often they will do their hunting separately keeping in touch with each other by vocalisation. Ocelots though basically terrestrial are very good climbers and have even been reported to catch some of their prey in trees. Whilst they do most of their hunting at dawn and dusk they are normally nocturnal cats and will spend most of the day asleep in thick cover. They will readily enter water and are good swimmers.

Prey is normally chased and caught on the ground rather than surprised from ambush. The main items of the diet are small birds, small rodents, agoutis, hares and pacas. Many other animals are preyed on including monkeys, small deer, porcupines, reptiles and young peccaries. Domestic stock such as calves and poultry are also eaten but normally Ocelots will avoid human habitation.

Breeding

There does not appear to be a fixed breeding season in the wild because kittens are found at all times of the year. In captivity the most commonly recorded oestrous cycle is about fifteen days, other periods observed have been six weeks and four months, in the latter case it is possible that conception took place and that the foetus was re-absorbed, but there is no hard evidence for this. The oestrous period normally lasts for five or six days and mating will take place frequently.

The female makes her den either in a small cave in the rocks or in a hollow log, after the kittens are born, usually one, and very seldom more than two, the father helps to feed them by bringing food to the den. The parents do not separate after the birth, it is very probable that they will keep the same partners for life, however there is as yet, no conclusive evidence for this.

Development of Young

The kittens are born blind but fully furred, the colouration is the same as in the adults. The eyes open at about fifteen to eighteen days and by about seven weeks the young are eating solid food.

By the time that they are six weeks old they will weigh about 970 g. and when nine and a half weeks old they will weigh about 1,360 g. The milk canines are lost at about seven months and the other deciduous teeth shortly afterwards. The kittens will reach maturity at about two to two and a half years.

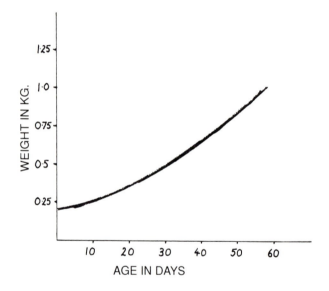

Weight gain recorded in an Ocelot Kitten

Status and Systematics

Throughout its range the Ocelot is pushed out by spreading human settlement and ruthlessly pursued by the fur trade because of its coat. All sub-species are classified as endangered.

Because it has 36 chromosomes, the hair on its neck is reversed, and it has an unusual eye socket formation the Ocelot is placed in the Genus *Leopardus* with some other South American cats.

There are generally considered to be eleven sub-species.

The International Species Indexing System numbers are as follows:-

1412007001020	Ocelot File Number	
1412007001020001	*Leopardus pardalis*	General Entry
1412007001020002	*Leopardus pardalis pardalis*	Veracruz - Honduras
1412007001020003	*Leopardus pardalis aequatorialis*	Peru - Costa Rica
1412007001020004	*Leopardus pardalis albescens*	Texas - Tamaulpia, Mexico
1412007001020005	*Leopardus pardalis maripensis*	Orinoco - Amazon Basin
1412007001020006	*Leopardus pardalis mearnsi*	Panama - Nicaragua
1412007001020007 -	*Leopardus pardalis mitis*	East Central Brazil North Argentina
1412007001020008	*Leopardus pardalis nelsoni*	Sinaloa - Oaxaca
1412007001020009	*Leopardus pardalis pseudopardalis*	North Venezuela - North Colombia
1412007001020010	*Leopardus pardalis pusea*	South West Ecuador
1412007001020011	*Leopardus pardalis sonoriensis*	Arizona - Sinoloa, Mexico
1412007001020012	*Leopardus pardalis steinbachi*	Central Bolivia

Chapter Twenty-five

MARGAY
Leopardus wiedi Schinz 1821

Vital Statistics

Length	head and body	male 53 - 79 cm.
		female 46 - 59 cm.
	tail	male 33 - 51 cm.
		female 34 - 44 cm.
Weight		male 5.0 kg.
		female 3.2 kg.
Age at maturity		approx. 2 years
Dental formula		$I\,^3/_3$ $C\,^1/_1$ $P\,^3/_2$ $M\,^1/_1$
Chromosome count		36
Karyotype		5 (Robinson)
Longevity		up to 13 years
Gestation period		80 - 85 days
Number of young		1 exceptionally 2
Weight at birth		80 - 125 g.
Age weaned		approx. 8 weeks

Description

The Margay resembles the Ocelot in colouring and coat pattern, however it is much smaller and has a very much longer tail. The hair on the back of the neck runs forward, from the inner corners of the eyes two stripes run over the top of the head, on the forehead these are joined by other stripes and all of them run down to the nape of the neck, there they become the start of rows of black spots which run along the sides and back of the body. The ground colour of the coat varies from shades of grey through ochre to tawny. The underside varies from yellow to white.

The eyes are very large and expressive with white streaks alongside the nose. The backs of the ears have white centres bordered by black and the tail is ringed with black for all of its length. Melanistic specimens are not recorded. The female has only one pair of teats.

Distribution and Habitat

The Margay is found in southern Texas, most of Mexico and all of Central America. In South America it is found in Colombia, Peru, North East Paraguay, Uruguay and some of North Argentina.

The Margay is exclusively a forest dweller and is found in all types of forest.

Habits

The Margay is extremely arboreal in its habits and spends the greater part of its life in the trees, it can run and jump from tree to tree almost in the manner of a monkey. It can even run along underneath branches and has been known to dangle from vines using only its hind legs to hang on by. One adaptation to life in the trees is its ability to turn its hind legs inwards through 180 degrees. Unlike other cats it is able to run headfirst down trees.

Basically the Margay is a solitary cat whose pattern of life is mostly diurnal, the opposite to what one might expect from the size of its eyes, it may be that exceptional eyesight is necessary for high speed manoeuvring in the tree tops. It is not known whether Margays hold territory in the wild, they certainly communicate using the odour of urine though. The fact that males bury their faeces may mean that they are not required to use them as territorial markers. Captive Margays will sometimes attempt to cover food that is not eaten immediately.

Eight different vocalisations have been identified indicating conditions of suspicion, threat, aggression, hunger and greeting, some calls have more intensity or urgency than others.

The range of animals taken as prey includes rodents, birds, lizards, tree frogs, squirrels, possums and monkeys. The method of hunting usually adopted is not known but in some cases stalking has been observed, it is probable that most prey is caught in the trees.

Breeding

As with most tropical cats there does not appear to be a fixed breeding season in the wild and the same situation is seen in captivity. The whole oestrous cycle appears to last approximately five weeks whilst the actual oestrous period lasts about one week. During oestrous the female indulges in a great deal of head rubbing on branches and in other prominent places. The male tests her readiness to mate by sniffing her genital area, whilst doing so he utters a low moaning sound like that of muted aggression. Copulation frequently takes place in the trees and is of very short duration, it is however repeated very often.

It is not known where the female gives birth in the wild but in captivity she will, if given the choice, give birth in a nest box high above the ground.

Development of Young

The kitten, very rarely are there two, is fully furred at birth, is darker than its parents and is blind. The eyes open at about eleven days old at which time the kitten starts to groom itself. Normally it starts to leave the nest at about five weeks old, during the time that it is within the nest the average daily gain in weight is about sixteen grams.

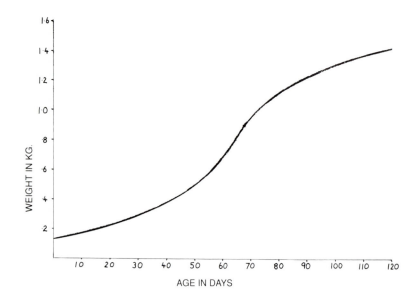

Average weight gain in Margay Kittens

The deciduous teeth are usually shed by about five months, however the kitten begins to take solid food around the eighth week. Adult weight is reached at about nine months in females and about twenty months in males. It is not known when Margays become independent in the wild but observations in captivity seem to suggest that it is at the approximate age of ten months.

Status and Systematics

Throughout its range the Margay is endangered, both by being poached for its fur, and more disastrously, through deforestation which affects it more than any other species of cat.

The Margay is usually assigned to the Genus *Leopardus* as a result of several characteristics that it shares with some other South American cats. There are usually considered to be eleven sub-species.

The International Species Indexing System numbers are as follows:-

1412007001030	Margay File Number	
1412007001030001	*Leopardus wiedi*	General Entry
1412007001030002	*Leopardus wiedi wiedi*	East Central Brazil North Argentina
1412007001030003	*Leopardus wiedi amazonica*	Amazonas, Brazil
1412007001030004	*Leopardus wiedi boliviae*	Bolivia - Mato Grosso, Brazil
1412007001030005	*Leopardus wiedi cooperi*	Nuevo Leon, Mexico - Texas
1412007001030006	*Leopardus wiedi glaucula*	Sinaloa - North Oaxaca
1412007001030007	*Leopardus wiedi nicaraguae*	Honduras - Costa Rica
1412007001030008	*Leopardus wiedi oaxacensis*	Tamaulipas - Oaxaca, Mexico
1412007001030009	*Leopardus wiedi pirrensis*	Panama - North Peru
1412007001030010	*Leopardus wiedi salvinia*	Chiapas, Guatemala - El Salvador
1412007001030011	*Leopardus wiedi yucatanica*	North Chiapas, North Guatemala - Yucatan Peninsula

Chapter Twenty-six

ONCILLA, LITTLE SPOTTED CAT
Leopardus tigrinus Schreber 1775

Vital Statistics

Length	head and body	40 - 55 cm.
	tail	25 - 40 cm.
Weight		male 2.75 kg.
		female 1.6 kg.
Dental formula		$I\,^3/_3$ $C\,^1/_1$ $P\,^3/_2$ $M\,^1/_1$
Chromosome count		36
Karyotype		4 (Robinson)
Gestation period		73 - 78 days
Number of young		1 - 2
Weight at birth		90 - 136 g.
Age weaned		approx. 8 weeks

Description

This cat is one of the smallest of the South American cats. The ground colour of the coat varies from light to rich ochre and is marked with rows of dark spots which appear as ringed blotches, these are smaller than those of the Margay. The colouring is lighter on the underside and the fur is very short and firm, the tail is ringed and tipped with black. The head is elongated and the eyes are fairly small, there is less tendency in this species to have facial stripes than in most other cats. Melanistic individuals have frequently been recorded.

Distribution and Habitat

The Oncilla is found throughout Central America and the northern parts of South America, it ranges from Costa Rica to northern Argentina but is not present in Chile or Bolivia. The preferred habitat is forests and bush country.

Habits

Little is known of the habits of this cat in the wild, it is known to be a good climber, although unlike the Margay it cannot descend trees head first. The prey consists of small mammals, birds, lizards and large insects.

Breeding and Development of Young

The Oncilla probably does not have a fixed breeding season in the wild, in captivity births are concentrated between February and August. It is not known what type of den the female prefers to give birth in.

The kittens are born fully furred and open their eyes sometime after the eighth day. They start eating solid food sometime during their sixth week. One strange feature is that the teeth, instead of appearing gradually, erupt all at once, between the second and third week. It would appear from the evidence of individuals hand-reared in captivity that this species has exceptionally high nutritional energy requirements, it is possible that this only applies to the kittens.

Status and Systematics

This species is thought to be very rare and is possibly endangered.

There are usually thought to be three sub-species.

The International Species Indexing System numbers are as follows:-

1412007001028	Oncilla File Number	
1412007001028001	*Leopardus tigrinus*	General Entry
1412007001028002	*Leopardus tigrinus tigrinus*	East Venezuela - North East Brazil
1412007001028003	*Leopardus tigrinus guttula*	East Central Brazil
1412007001028004	*Leopardus tigrinus pardinoides*	West Venezuela - West Ecuador

Chapter Twenty-seven

GEOFFROY'S CAT
Leopardus geoffroyi d'Orbigny and Gervais 1843

Vital Statistics

Length	head and body	45 - 70 cm.
	tail	26 - 55 cm.
Height at shoulder		15 - 22.5 cm.
Weight		2.2 - 5 kg.
Age at maturity		approx. 2½ years
Dental formula		$I^3/_3$ $C^1/_1$ $P^3/_2$ $M^1/_1$
Chromosome count		36
Karyotype		4 (Robinson)
Longevity		up to 16 years
Gestation period		72 -78 days
Number of young		1 - 4
Weight at birth		65 - 90g.
Age weaned		approx. 9 weeks

Description

A slender little cat scarcely bigger than a Domestic Cat. The ground colour of the coat varies from silver grey for individuals in the South to yellow ochre for those in the North, every possible shade in-between is also found. On the flanks and back there are black spots which are all of nearly equal size, on the chest these spots merge to form stripes. There are black stripes on the cheeks and on the forehead, those on the forehead run over the head to the back of the neck. In some individuals there is a partial dorsal stripe towards the shoulders. The tail is spotted at the base and ringed towards the tip. The backs of the ears are black with large white central patches. Melanistic individuals are reported frequently. The female normally has two pairs of teats.

Distribution

This species is found in South America from Bolivia in the centre to the Rio Gallego in the far South. Individuals have even been found around the Straits of Magellan making this cat (together with the Puma) the most southerly occurring species of cat in the world. It is rarely found in Chile except occasionally in the high Andes. In Brazil it is only found in the South West.

Habitat

Within its range this cat occupies a wide variety of country varying from the dry salt desert of western Argentina to the lush grasslands of the pampas. It is frequently found in scrubland where there are small trees and shrubs such as Mesquite. Geoffroy's Cat occurs from sea level up to altitudes of 3,500 metres, the preferred territory appears to be in mountainous areas.

Habits

This species has been little studied in the wild but certain things can be deduced from observations in captivity, these tell us that this cat is largely tree dwelling and they are reported as sleeping in trees at night. It is a very agile climber and is reported to catch some of its prey in the trees, observations on some individuals show that they are good swimmers.

The pattern of movement of Geoffroy's Cat shows that it is crepuscular with a preference for evening rather than morning activity. It is very secretive and seldom approaches human habitation. A sub-adult female who was tracked in the wild using a radio collar turned out to have a home range of 2.8 square kilometres. Since adults in the cat family often have a smaller range than sub-adults it is possible that in a suitable habitat there may be a large number of these cats. It is not known if the territory is marked in the wild but in captivity faeces are deposited around the perimeter fence of the enclosure, frequently these are deposited high above the ground with the same sites being used repeatedly. No pattern has been observed to their urination.

The range of vocalization shown by this species is quite extensive and includes:- hissing, spitting, growling, purring, a medium pitched moaning sound and a short sharp sound that resembles a hurried version of a Domestic Cat's "mew". When the female is in oestrous a high pitched wailing sound has been heard.

The range of prey is known to include:- tuco-tuco, rats, mice, guinea pigs and agoutis, small birds and tree dwelling lizards are also eaten. Hunting is said to be done by hiding in shrubs and trees and ambushing the prey in the same manner as the Jaguar.

Breeding

Observations in captivity show that Geoffroy's Cat has a definite breeding season, in the wild the breeding season is between June and December. Captive animals in the northern hemisphere also come into oestrous in the Spring. It appears that the female comes into oestrous every twenty-four to twenty-eight days. During oestrous the female will eat less than usual and will indulge in much head rubbing against prominent tree trunks and rocks in order to spread the scent from her facial glands. Copulation may take place either in the trees or on the ground, after mating the pair will go their separate ways and the male will take no part in the raising of the kittens.

The female gives birth in a well protected den concealed amongst rocks or in dense shrubs. In captivity if the female is given a choice she will give birth in a nest box above ground level, this may indicate that in the wild she chooses, whenever possible, a site high up which is less easily reached by predators. The kittens may number from one to four, with two and one being the most common. If for any reason the kittens do not survive the female will come back into oestrous as little as ten days after their loss.

Development of Young

The kittens are born blind and start to open their eyes at about ten to twelve days of age, they will be fully focusing at about three weeks. Teething starts at around six days old but it is not known when it is completed, the kittens are however able to eat solid food when six to seven weeks old.

Development of movement is rapid; the kittens can lift their own weight off the ground for short period when four days old and they start to emerge from the den at about five weeks. When they are six weeks old they are able to climb in a very agile manner and appear to have no fear of heights. From observations made in captivity it appears that they become independent after about eight months and that they become mature at about two and a half to three years old.

Status and Systematics

Whilst the status of Geoffroy's Cat in the wild is uncertain it is inferred from capture records that the species is vulnerable and becoming endangered.

Geoffroy's Cat was at one time classified together with the Oncilla and the Kodkod in a separate Genus *Oncifelis* however nowadays it is usually placed in the Genus *Leopardus* whose chief distinction is that it has 36 chromosomes. Five sub-species are recognised, one of these, *salinarum* was until recently classed as a fully separate species.

The International Species Indexing System numbers are as follows:-

1412007001010	Geoffroy's Cat File Number	
1412007001010001	*Leopardus geoffroyi*	General Entry
1412007001010002	*Leopardus geoffroyi geoffroyi*	Central Argentina
1412007001010003	*Leopardus geoffroyi euxantha*	Bolivia
1412007001010004	*Leopardus geoffroyi leucobapta*	Patagonia
1412007001010005	*Leopardus geoffroyi paraguayae*	North Argentina
1412007001010006	*Leopardus geoffroyi salinarum*	North West - Central Argentina

Chapter Twenty-eight

KODKOD
Leopardus guigna Molina 1782

Vital Statistics

Length	head and body	39 - 50 cm.
	tail	19 - 23 cm.
Weight		2 - 3 kg.
Dental formula	$I\,^{3}/_{3}$ $C\,^{1}/_{1}$	$P\,^{2(3)}/_{2}$ $M\,^{1}/_{1}$
Longevity		up to 11 years

Description

The Kodkod is a very small cat, one sub-species *(L.g. guigna)* is probably the smallest cat in the New World. The structure of the skull is like that of the Margay although the Kodkod usually has only twenty-eight teeth and has shorter legs. The ground colour of the coat is yellow ochre or grey-brown becoming whiter on the underside, the coat is covered with blackish spots on both back and flanks. There are stripes on the head and the front of the chest. The backs of the ears are black with white centres and the tail has black rings round it. The claws are larger than on other cats of about the same size. Melanistic individuals have been seen frequently.

The northern form is larger and paler while the southern form is smaller, more boldly marked and has spotted feet.

Distribution and Habitat

The range of the Kodkod is limited to Chile and the Andean lakes district of Argentina in Chubut and Santa Cruz provinces.

This cat is found in semi-open country where there are just a few shrubs and trees to give it cover, it is not present in grassland nor in the arid regions of the Atacama.

Habits

The few reports we have of this cat give a widely conflicting picture of its behaviour, the strong claws would seem to

Lion

Tiger

Jaguar

Leopard

Snow Leopard

Clouded Leopard

Ocelot

Margay

Oncilla

Pampas Cat

Caracal

Serval

African Golden Cat

Black-footed Cat

Geoffroy's Cat

Melanistic Geoffroy's Cat

Jaguarundi

Pallas's Cat

Rusty Spotted Cat

Lynx

Flat Headed Cat

Leopard Cat

European Wild Cat

Fishing Cat

Cheetah

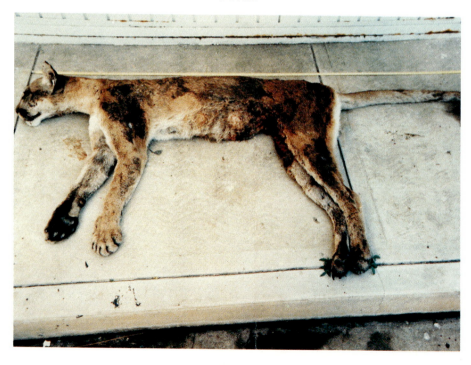

Onza

indicate that it is a good climber, however reports of captive animals suggest they spend most of their time on the ground. In the wild the Kodkod appears to be nocturnal but in captivity most of the activity takes place by day. A report of this species raiding henhouses in parties suggests that it may be gregarious but it is not known if this was normal behaviour. It may be conjectured that they eat small mammals in the wild, the rest of their diet is unknown apart from their raiding of domestic poultry.

Status and Systematics

The Kodkod is common in the district around Valdivia but its status elsewhere is unknown.

This species was at one time thought to be identical with Geoffroy's Cat and has at various times been assigned to three different genera. Nowadays it is generally included in the Genus *Leopardus*, although Hemmer puts it in the Genus *Oncifelis*, together with the Geoffroy's Cat and the Oncilla. There are two sub-species.

The International Species Indexing System numbers are as follows:-

1412007001011	Kodkod File Number	
1412007001011001	*Leopardus guigna*	General Entry
1412007001011002	*Leopardus guigna guigna*	Patagonia, South Chile
1412007001011003	*Leopardus guigna tigrillo*	Central Chile

Chapter Twenty-nine

PAMPAS CAT
Lynchailurus colocolo Molina 1782

Vital Statistics

Length	head and body	55 - 70 cm.
	tail	29 - 32 cm.
Height at shoulder		30 - 35 cm.
Weight		4 - 7 kg.
Age at maturity		approx. 2 years
Dental formula		$I \frac{3}{3}$ $C \frac{1}{1}$ $P \frac{2}{2}$ $M \frac{1}{1}$
Chromosome count		36
Karyotype		4 (Robinson)
Longevity		up to 13 years
Gestation period		80 - 85 days
Number of young		1 - 3

Description

A stocky little cat about the same size as a Domestic Cat but much more robustly built with a short round head and a fairly short tail, it has a broad face and pointed ears. Those individuals in the South of the range have ears with grey backs whilst those in the North have ears with black backs and grizzled centres.

The ground colour of the coat is silvery-grey with reddish brown elongated blotches running diagonally, sometimes these merge to form stripes. The underside is whitish and there are prominent brown bars on the legs and fainter ones on the tail. Bars run from the eyes to the front of the ears, individuals from the West are more strongly marked than those from the East. On the muzzle there are two very prominent spots alongside the nostrils. The tail has a bushy appearance and the rest of the fur is long and luxurious. Melanistic specimens are well known and have been seen in captivity.

Distribution and Habitat

The Pampas Cat is widely distributed in South America and

is present in Chile, Peru, Brazil (Mato Grosso), Bolivia, Paraguay, Uruguay, Ecuador and Argentina as far South as Patagonia. Throughout its range it is found inland and does not frequent the coast.

Through most of its range this species lives in grasslands and country where there are thickets to give it extra protection, some animals in the northern parts of the range will enter humid forests.

Habits

The Pampas Cat is solitary by nature and is almost exclusively nocturnal, it is said to be entirely terrestrial although one cat known to the author spent all its time up in the trees. From its behaviour in captivity it may be deduced that the territory of an individual covers a large area, in captivity this cat has not been known to mark its territory.

The prey consists of small mammals, especially guinea pigs, and also ground dwelling birds, from the fact that it is an untidy jumper (although accurate) we might deduce that it seldom employs ambush.

Breeding and Development of Young

All the births recorded in captivity have taken place in April and July, one wild female who was examined at post-mortem, also in April, had a small foetus on which the hair was just forming. It seems possible therefore that there is no fixed breeding season for this species. It is usually stated that up to three kittens may be born, however in all the recorded cases there has only been one offspring. Nothing else is known about the breeding, or development of the young.

Status and Systematics

Whilst there are places where it is locally common the Pampas Cat is regarded as rare throughout its range.

Because it has certain aberrant characteristics the Pampas Cat is placed by itself in a separate Genus *Lynchailurus;* Hemmer classifies this as a sub-genus, in the Genus *Oncifelis.*

There are seven sub-species.

The International Species Indexing System numbers are as follows:-

1412007001008	Pampas Cat File Number	
1412007001008001	*Lynchailurus colocolo*	General Entry
1412007001008002	*Lynchailurus colocolo colocolo*	Central Chile
1412007001008003	*Lynchailurus colocolo braccata*	Central Brazil
1412007001008004	*Lynchailurus colocolo budini*	North-West Argentina
1412007001008005	*Lynchailurus colocolocrespoi*	North-West Argentina
1412007001008006	*Lynchailurus colocolo garleppi*	South Peru, West Bolivia
1412007001008007	*Lynchailurus colocolo pajeros*	Central Argentina
1412007001008008	*Lynchailurus colocolo thomasi*	Ecuador, North Peru

Chapter Thirty

ANDEAN MOUNTAIN CAT, ANDEAN HIGHLAND CAT
Oreailurus jacobita Cornalia 1865

Vital Statistics

Length	head and body	60 - 80 cm.
	tail	35 - 50 cm.
Dental formula	$I^3/_3$ $C^1/_1$ $P^3/_2$ $M^1/_1$	
Weight		3 - 7 kg.

Description

The Andean Mountain Cat is frequently confused with the Pampas Cat, it has very much the same thick fur, about four centimetres long on the back and about three and a half centimetres long on the tail. The ground colour of the coat is silver-grey turning to ash brown on the back and getting whitish on the underside. Spots are arranged in diagonal lines on the coat and are black on the belly and legs shading to brown or orange-yellow on the back. On the tail there are brown ochre rings and the backs of the ears are grey.

The skull of this cat differs from all others in having very peculiar double chambered bullae.

Distribution and Habitat

The Andean Mountain Cat is found in South America and is limited to the highland areas of Peru, Bolivia, Argentina and Chile. Generally this species keeps to the arid and semi-arid regions living and hunting above the tree line sometimes at altitudes of more than five thousand metres.

Habits

This species is seldom seen and so almost nothing is known of its life in the wild. The prey is known to include Chinchillas and Viscachas and it probably eats other rodents as well. Some reports say that it enters the snow regions occasionally, but the reasons for this are not known.

Status and Systematics

This cat is thought to be rare throughout its range.

There is only one sub-species thought to exist.

The International Species Indexing System Numbers are as follows:-

1412007001013	Andean Mountain Cat File Number	
1412007001013001	*Oreailurus jacobita jacobita*	West and Central South America

Chapter Thirty-one

PUMA, COUGAR
Puma concolor Linnaeus 1771

Vital Statistics

Length	head and body	male 105 - 196 cm.
		female 95 -150 cm.
	tail	male 66 - 78 cm.
		female 53 - 81 cm.
Height at shoulder		60 - 76 cm.
Weight		male 67 - 103 kg.
		female 36 - 60 kg.
Age at maturity		approx. 2 years
Dental formula		$I \, ^3/_3$ $C \, ^1/_1$ $P \, ^3/_2$ $M \, ^1/_1$
Chromosome count		38
Karyotype		2 (Robinson)
Longevity		up to 19 years
Gestation period		93 - 98 days
Number of young		1 - 6
Weight at birth		226 - 453 g.
Age weaned		approx. 10 weeks

Description

A large cat with a long tail, the Puma has a plain coat with no obvious markings, the colouration is a shade of grey which varies from medium to light, some individuals have a coat which is a shade of red, this too varies from foxy to deep tawny. There is a tendency for reddish animals to be more common in warmer parts of the range and for grey animals to be more common in cooler places. Similarly the larger individuals occur in the cooler parts of the range and the smaller ones in the warmer parts of the range. The underparts of the body are whitish whilst the sides of the muzzle are black, the backs of the ears are also black and sometimes have lighter coloured patches in their centres.

Juveniles have a distinctly spotted coat with a ringed tail, this pattern is kept until they are about half grown. Melanistic Pumas have occasionally been seen in Central and South America, they have never been reported from North America.

Distribution

The Puma was formerly found throughout southern Canada also through the whole of North, Central and South America as far as the Straits of Magellan.

Today the Puma is absent from much of eastern Canada and the Central and eastern United States. Scattered remnants of the former population may be found in the following places, Florida, Georgia, the southern Appalachians, New York, New Jersey, Maine, New Brunswick and Nova Scotia. In the West of the United States and Canada it is still quite prolific, there are recent reports of Pumas being found within the boundaries of the city of Edmonton. It is still persecuted in South America and in some places is consequently becoming difficult to find.

Habitat

The Puma can cope with a great variety of different conditions including, tropical rain forest, pine forest, swampy jungle, grassland and scrub. About the only type of terrain that it actively shuns is desert, all the Puma needs is cover, water and something to eat. This species has been recorded at sea-level and also at an altitude of 4,500 metres.

Habits

The Puma is a naturally secretive animal whose normal pattern of movement is nocturnal, in areas where they have nothing to fear from man they are sometimes seen at twilight and at times when food is scarce they may do their hunting in daylight.

Pumas are territorial animals and males will occupy a large territory and be very scrupulous in avoiding each other. The size of the territory varies with the type of country and may be as large as four hundred and fifty square kilometres. The resident animal will visit every part of the territory on a regular basis, these visits may be fifteen to eighteen days apart. Females live more closely together and there may be several female territories within that of the male. It also appears that territories of females will overlap each other. Territories are marked by scraping up little dung hills, these are renewed every time the animal passes, other Pumas passing by will smell the fresh scent and keep out of the way. As well as resident animals the Puma population contains nomads who are usually newly adult individuals looking for a territory of their own to occupy. These nomads may travel as much as forty kilometres in a single night whilst seeking a home. Since the suitable habitat is usually already occupied there is a high mortality rate amongst nomads.

For food the Puma is prepared to eat anything that it can catch, grasshoppers are eaten as are bison and young bears. The mainstay of their diet, when available is deer, these they kill by leaping from ambush and breaking their necks. In some cases they will chase their prey on the ground and one account describes a Puma chasing monkeys from tree to tree among the branches. Since Pumas have been known to attack prey up to six times their own weight they sometimes fall victim themselves, there are reports of Puma being killed by Wapiti (*Cervus canadensis*) defending their calves.

Pumas are very agile and are good swimmers, they have been reported making jumps of twelve metres long while running, and jumping four metres vertically into trees. Apart from Wolves (*Canis* sps.) Pumas have no enemies except man, who hunts them with dog packs. When chased most Pumas will take to the trees and remain there until nightfall, but the Vancouver Island sub-species is said to attack the dogs and to refuse to stay in a tree long enough to be shot at.

Breeding

There does not appear to be a fixed breeding season but in temperate climes most births take place in the Spring and Summer. The female is in oestrous for between eight and eleven days, the inter-oestrous period is three to four weeks. During oestrous the female gives out horrendous screams which sound like those of an alley cat greatly amplified. The pair stay together only a short time and the female may mate with other males. The den where the female gives birth is in a protected site usually amongst rocks, and is sometimes lined with moss, caves are also used frequently. The number of kittens varies between one and five, though exceptionally there may be six. It is probable that only those females who occupy territories are able to breed.

The composition of the maternal milk is as follows:-

Water	65%
Fat	18.6%
Protein	12%
Carbohydrate	6.9%
Ash	1%

Development of Young

The kittens are born blind but fully furred, the eyes open well before the end of the second week. They begin to eat meat at about six weeks and by the end of their sixth month they are accompanying their mother on hunting expeditions. The male takes no part in the rearing of the young.

At the end of twenty months the young are driven away by their mother to become nomads in search of a territory of their own. Sub-adults may disperse over one hundred kilometres before being able to find a territory of their own.

Status and Systematics

In most parts of its range the Puma is at present considered to be vulnerable, some sub-species however are increasing their numbers. The main threats to the species come from ranchers who consider it a threat to their livestock, and from the clearance of land for crops.

Many different sub-species have been described in the past, some of these are now considered to be synonyms. Currently there are considered to be twenty-nine sub-species.

The International Species Indexing System Numbers are as follows:-

1412007001009	Puma File Number	
1412007001009001	*Puma concolor*	General Entry
1412007001009002	*Puma concolor concolor*	Venezuela, Guyana, Brazil
1412007001009003	*Puma concolor acrocodia*	South West Mato Grosso, Bolivia, North Argentina
1412007001009004	*Puma concolor anthonyi*	South Venezuela
1412007001009005	*Puma concolor araucana*	Chile, Argentina
1412007001009006	*Puma concolor azteca*	Arizona, New Mexico - Mexico City

1412007001009007	*Puma concolor bangsi*	West Columbia - West Ecuador
1412007001009008	*Puma concolor borbensis*	Amazonas Ecuador
1412007001009009	*Puma concolor browni*	Hualpi Mountains Catavina, Baja
1412007001009010	*Puma concolor cabrerae*	West and Central Argentina
1412007001009011	*Puma concolor californica*	California - North Baja
1412007001009012	*Puma concolor capricornensis*	South-East Brazil - North Argentina
1412007001009013	*Puma concolor coryi*	Arkansas - Louisiana - Florida
1412007001009014	*Puma concolor costaricensis*	Nicaragua - Panama
1412007001009015	*Puma concolor cougar*	Tennessee - East Michigan
1412007001009016	*Puma concolor greeni*	East Brazil - South Amazonas
1412007001009017	*Puma concolor hippolestes*	North Dakota - Wyoming Colorado and Alberta
1412007001009018	*Puma concolor hudsoni*	South Central Argentina
1412007001009019	*Puma concolor improcera*	South Baja, California
1412007001009020	*Puma concolor incarum*	North Peru, South Ecuador
1412007001009021	*Puma concolor kaibabensis*	Nevada, Utah, North Arizona
1412007001009022	*Puma concolor mayensis*	Guerro Vera., Mexico, Honduras
1412007001009023	*Puma concolor missoulensis*	British Columbia, Alberta, Idaho, Montana
1412007001009024	*Puma concolor oregonensis*	South East British Columbia, Washington, Oregon
1412007001009025	*Puma concolor osgoodi*	Central Eastern Bolivia
1412007001009026	*Puma concolor pearsoni*	Patagonia, South Chile

1412007001009027	*Puma concolor puma*	Central Chile, West Argentina
1412007001009028	*Puma concolor schorgeri*	Minnesota, Wisconsin, Kansas, Missouri
1412007001009029	*Puma concolor stanleyana*	Oklahoma, Texas - North East Mexico
1412007001009030	*Puma concolor vancouverensis*	Vancouver Island

Some authorities also list as valid sub-species the following:-

| *Puma concolor olympus* | Washington |
| *Puma concolor soderstromi* | Ecuador |

Chapter Thirty-Two

MARBLED CAT
Pardofelis marmorata Martin 1836

Vital Statistics

Length	head and body	46 - 60 cm.
	tail	35 - 41 cm.
Weight		approx. 5.5 kg.
Age at maturity		approx. 21 months
Dental formula		$I\,^3/_3 \quad C\,^1/_1 \quad P\,^{2(3)}/_2 \quad M\,^1/_1$
Chromosome count		38
Gestation period		approx. 81 days
Number of young		1 - 4
Weight at birth		approx. 100 g.

Description

A small sized cat with a long tail and fairly large ears. The texture of the fur is very soft and on the flanks it has a mottled appearance. The ground colour varies from greyish brown to ochre or ruddy brown, the patterning consists of large blotches of a darker colour outlined in black, there are black spots over the top of the head, on the chest, on the legs and at the base of the tail. The tail is ringed with black towards its tip, the underparts of the throat and body are lighter than the back. The backs of the ears are black with a lighter centre.

Usually the first upper premolar is absent, when present it is very small.

Distribution

The Marbled Cat is confined to southern Asia. It is found in Nepal, and thence eastwards through Assam, Burma, Thailand, the Malayan Peninsula, Sumatra and Borneo.

Habitat and Habits

The Marbled Cat lives in the forest and is thought to be largely arboreal, there is a report of an individual hunting birds in the trees. It appears to be mainly nocturnal, known prey includes rats, squirrels and birds with the possible addition of lizards and frogs.

One peculiarity of its behaviour is that it almost always adopts an arched back position whether sitting or standing. It has been generally found to be a very fierce animal.

Breeding and Development of the Young

Nothing is known of this species breeding in the wild but a small amount is known from animals that have been bred in captivity. From the fact that captive births took place in January, February and September it appears that there is no fixed breeding season.

The kittens are born blind and fully furred, the coat although mottled has no definite pattern, the eyes open at around two weeks old. At two and a half weeks the deciduous teeth start to appear and the kittens attempt to walk, at three weeks old they are fully alert for sight and sound. The deciduous teeth are fully erupted by the fifth week and the kittens are then very active. At six and a half weeks the marbled pattern starts to appear in the coat and is complete by about four months old, at which time the milk canines are shed.

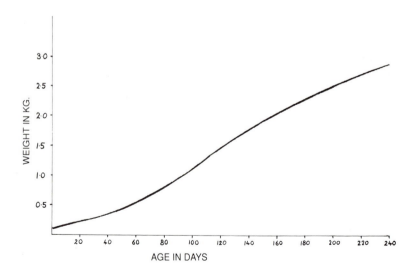

Weight gain recorded in a Marbled Cat Kitten

Status and Systematics

Although the Marbled Cat is thought to be rare it has not been possible to obtain an estimate of its numbers, in the absence of any definite information it must be considered as vulnerable.

Whilst the Marbled Cat shows many features of the small cats the chromosomes appear to be closest to those of the Tiger, therefore it is placed in a Genus of its own, *Pardofelis*. There are considered to be two sub-species.

The International Species Indexing System numbers are as follows:-

1412007001018	Marbled Cat File Number	
1412007001018001	*Pardofelis marmorata*	General Entry
1412007001018002	*Pardofelis marmorata marmorata*	Malaya - Borneo
1412007001018003	*Pardofelis marmorata charltoni*	Nepal - Burma

Chapter Thirty-three

CLOUDED LEOPARD
Neofelis nebulosa Griffith 1821

Vital Statistics

Length	head and body	80 - 105 cm.
	tail	70 - 90 cm.
Height at shoulder		approx. 53 cm.
Weight		22 kg.
Dental formula		$I\,^3/_3$ $C\,^1/_1$ $P\,^3/_2$ $M\,^1/_1$
Chromosome count		38
Karyotype		1 (Robinson)
Longevity		up to 17 years
Gestation period		86 - 92 days
Number of young		2 - 3
Weight at birth		145 - 170g.
Age weaned		8 - 9 weeks
Age at maturity		females 3 years
		males 4 years

Description

This species which is of medium to large size is one of those which bridge the gap between the large and small cats. Whilst the hyoid arch is fully ossified, a characteristic of small cats, the pupil of the eye is spindled; round pupils are generally a characteristic of big cats, and split pupils are a characteristic of small cats. The Clouded Leopard has a long body, fairly short legs and a long tail (except for the Taiwanese sub-species). The ground colour of the coat varies from pale ochre through varying shades of russet to rich brown, on the flank there are large patches approximately rectangular in shape which are of deeper colour, these are outlined in black. The undersides are white with black blotches on the belly, legs and throat; the tail has black spots which are so close as to appear like rings round it while the tip is black. Rows of spots run from above the eyes over the head to the nape of the neck, sometimes these merge together to form stripes, there are two broad stripes on each cheek and the backs of the ears are black with grey patches in the centre. The canine teeth are extremely large and more slender than their length would suggest.

Distribution

The Clouded Leopard is found in South-East Asia and ranges from Nepal, Sikkim and Bhutan in the Himalayas, through the hills of Assam into Burma, Thailand and Malaya. It is also found through Indo-china and in mainland China as far North as Fukien. Island forms occur in Taiwan, Hainan, Borneo and Sumatra, there are also reports that it may be present on Iriomotejima.

Habitat

Within its range the Clouded Leopard is a forest dweller, occurring in dense evergreen forest and in secondary forest. It is found everywhere from near sea level to altitudes of 2,400 metres.

Habits

At one time it was thought that this species was largely nocturnal and whilst captive individuals show this pattern recent studies have shown it to be largely crepuscular in the wild. While Clouded Leopards are thought to be solitary animals there are enough reports of pairs being found together to make us treat such thoughts with caution. The Clouded Leopard is an extremely agile climber, it has been seen to hunt monkeys in the treetops and to ambush its prey by hiding in the trees. It is so accomplished that it can run down trees head first like a Margay. In spite of such agility it spends much of its waking time on the ground (where it also does most of its hunting), retiring to the trees to sleep.

The most characteristic sound made by the adult is a sort of moaning roar, the youngsters chuckle, purr and growl. The prey includes monkeys, squirrels and birds; sheep and goats, both domestic and wild, are also eaten, however the preferred prey when available consists of deer and wild boar.

Breeding

Whilst almost nothing is known of the breeding behaviour of this species in the wild, some breeding has taken place in captivity and therefore some deductions can be made. Captive breeding has taken place at all times of the year, although a peak in births occurs in early spring. While oestrus is usually said to last between three and nine days studies in Thailand have revealed that it may last as little as one day, during this time copulation takes place three to five times.

During oestrous the female increases her vocalizations by a considerable amount and the male, when in her vicinity indulges in a lot of head rubbing. In captivity mating has been observed between individuals who were eighteen months old. Gestation lasts between 86 and 92 days.

In the wild the female conceals the kittens in a den which is made on the ground in dense jungle cover. Captive females will exhibit a desire for privacy during birth which is far more extreme than that shown in any other cat. Should the kittens be lost for any reason the female will enter oestrous again approximately twenty-five days later.

Development of Young

The kittens are born blind and fully furred, the coat colour differs from that of the adults in that the interior of the blotches on the flanks is almost black. The kittens open their eyes at about twelve days and whilst they are able to move about at three weeks they do not leave the den until they are about five weeks old. The kittens are able to romp and play when they are about six weeks old and when they are eleven weeks old they are eating solid meat. However it is usually not until they are around eighteen weeks old that they kill their own prey. It is believed that they become independent at about nine months old.

The male gains weight faster than the female, so that while at about six weeks they both weigh about one kilogram, by the time that they reach eight months the male will weigh about twelve kilograms and the female about seven and a half kilograms.

Status and Systematics

The Clouded Leopard is rare throughout its range and in some areas it is seriously endangered through the rapid destruction of its habitat. Because of the characteristics of its skull it is placed in a Genus of its own, *Neofelis*, there are usually considered to be four subspecies.

The International Species Indexing System Numbers are as follows:-

1412007002002	Clouded Leopard File Number	
1412007002002001	*Neofelis nebulosa*	General Entry
1412007002002002	*Neofelis nebulosa nebulosa*	South China and Indochina
1412007002002003	*Neofelis nebulosa brachyurus*	Taiwan
1412007002002004	*Neofelis nebulosa diardi*	Borneo
1412007002002005	*Neofelis nebulosa macrosceloides*	Nepal to Burma

Chapter Thirty-Four

SNOW LEOPARD, OUNCE
Uncia uncia Schreber 1775

Vital Statistics

Length	head and body	male approx. 1.3 metres
		female approx. 1.0 metres
	tail	male approx. 0.9 metres
		female approx. 0.8 metres
Height at shoulder		approx. 60 cm.
Weight		25 -75 kg.
Dental formula		$I\,^3/_3$ $C\,^1/_1$ $P\,^3/_2$ $M\,^1/_1$
Chromosome count		38
Karyotype		1 (Robinson)
Longevity		up to 15 years
Age at maturity		3 - 4 years
Gestation period		97 - 105 days
Number of young		1 - 4
Weight at birth		300 - 700 g.
Age weaned		approx. 3 months

Description

A large cat slightly smaller than the Leopard, the Snow Leopard or Ounce has a broad rounded head with a short skull and a wide expansion of the nasal cavity, the hyoid bone is only partly ossified but the species is nevertheless able to purr. The tail is relatively long. The ears are rounded and the backs are black at the tips and base with the centres a smoky grey colour.

The coat is luxuriously thick, the ground colour is grey with a yellowish tinge on the flanks while the belly is creamy white. On the back and the flanks there are black rosettes with open centres, these are interspersed with small black spots, the forehead has black spots which are arranged in lines reminiscent of the patterns in small cats. The tail is thickly furred and is marked with rosettes, the broad feet are also thickly furred thus acting as natural snow shoes. On young cubs the markings are strikingly coloured giving the young a strong resemblance to the young of the Puma, as the cat grows to adulthood the markings become less well defined.

Distribution and Habitat

The Ounce has a fairly restricted range situated in the mountains of Central Asia, it is found patchily distributed in the Soviet Union, China, India, Mongolia, Pakistan and Afghanistan. Within this area it is found on the lower slopes and foothills of the Himalayas up to altitudes of 4,300 metres above sea level.

Whilst the Ounce follows the game down into the valleys in Winter it seldom descends below 1,500 metres. It appears not to like living in a true forest habitat but prefers to keep to the arid regions amid the rocky wilderness and glaciers.

Habits

The Ounce is a terrestrial species which, within its territory makes great use of rocky clefts and caves, sometimes using the same den for years. In the Ala-Tau mountains of the Soviet Union they often use the nests of Black Vultures in Juniper trees both as resting places and as look-out platforms.

The size of the territory occupied by an Ounce is not known however it appears to be large. Ounces leave marks of scent and urine at well defined places within their territory, scrapes have been found both with and without faeces. They appear to use regular routes through their territories, this may be a method of keeping in touch with Ounces who hold neighbouring territories. Individuals who meet will greet each other with a low, almost inaudible, puffing sound which appears to be similar in function to the 'prusten' of Tigers.

References abound in the literature to 'resident pairs' of Ounces and, while adults may not spend all their time together, some form of pair bond may be established for life. It appears that territory is occupied by a single individual through the use of frequent marking.

While the Ounce is primarily a nocturnal animal examination of some of its kills indicates that they have been made in the daytime. This cat is an outstanding leaper and one jump, made over a ditch whilst running uphill, was measured as being sixteen metres.

111

The Ounce has a small range of vocalisations, of which the most frequently heard is a yowl, other sounds are a rumble, a hiss, a low growl and a roar, this last one has only been when used in anger. The choice of prey is dictated by the nature of the game available.

Breeding

In the wild Ounces appear to be seasonal breeders with mating occurring between February and April and births between May and July. It is thought that in the wild the females give birth every second year and that the young remain with her for more than twelve months.

Oestrous lasts for about six days and if the first litter is lost for any reason a further oestrous will occur seventeen to twenty-three days later. In the wild the male does not take part in the rearing of the cubs but in captivity males have been seen to play a full part in the rearing.

A survey of forty-seven litters conducted by Freeman (1977) revealed fourteen litters with one cub, twenty litters with two cubs, ten litters with three cubs and three litters with four cubs. The distribution of the sexes was, forty-six male cubs, forty-two female cubs and nine cubs whose sex was unknown.

Development of Young

The cubs are born in a cave or deep cleft in the rocks where the mother has been in seclusion for about a week previously. Parturition takes approximately two hours. When born the cubs are blind, fully furred and strongly marked miniatures of their parents.

During the first week after giving birth the female leaves the den only for the purpose of defecation, during the second week she begins to move about more frequently. The eyes of the cubs open when they are about eleven days old and their ears by the time that they are about two weeks old, during the first two weeks of their lives their behaviour is entirely mother orientated and consists wholly of feeding and sleeping. At between two and three weeks old the cubs stand and begin to walk, this is also when their social play behaviour starts. At this time also their teeth start to appear. The cubs begin to leave the den when they are around five or six weeks old and play progresses to include stalking and hunting behaviour.

Full weaning probably does not take place until they are about three months old. By the time they are five months old they are capable of jumping a barrier 1.27 metres high. In the wild they stay with their mother until they are more than a year old.

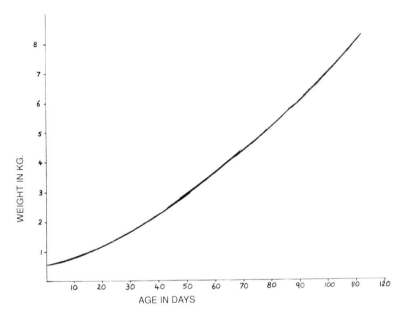

Average weight gain in Snow Leopard Cubs

Status and Systematics

The Ounce is rare throughout its range, because of the attentions of the fur trade its numbers declined throughout the nineteen seventies causing this species to be classified as endangered.

Although the hyoid bone is partially ossified the Ounce is nevertheless able to purr, and because of the characteristics of the skull, this species is considered sufficiently different from the other big cats to be classified in a Genus of its own, *Uncia*.

There is only one subspecies, the nominate one.

The International Species Indexing System numbers are as follows:-

1412007002006	Snow Leopard File Number	
1412007002006001	*Uncia uncia uncia*	Tibet, Himalaya, Mongolia

Chapter Thirty-five

LEOPARD
Panthera pardus Linnaeus 1758

Vital Statistics

Length	head and body	male 1.15 - 1.67 metres
		female 0.95 - 1.24 metres
	tail	0.58 - 0.96 metres
Height at shoulder		0.45 - 0.78 metres
Weight		35 - 54 kg.
Age at maturity		male 2 - 3 years
		female 2 years approx.
Dental formula		$I\,^3/_3$ $C\,^1/_1$ $P\,^3/_2$ $M\,^1/_1$
Chromosome count		38
Karyotype		1 (Robinson)
Longevity		up to 23 years
Gestation period		93 - 98 days
Number of young		1 - 4
Weight at birth		430 - 600 g.
Age weaned		approx. 3 months

Description

A big cat, the Leopard is in some ways the archetypal spotted cat, the ground colour of the coat varies from straw coloured to deep ochre and the depth of the pelage varies from short in the tropical sub-species to long and silky in those from cooler climates. The undersides of the throat, neck and belly are white as are the centres of the back of the ears. The back and flanks are covered with black spots arranged in rosettes which are frequently open in the centre, the spots are also to be seen in the tail where they become rings towards the tip. The chest is covered with spots arranged in the form of collar markings, these are usually short and broken. Melanistic individuals are found frequently and are often referred to as 'Black Panthers', cream coloured individuals and albinos are also found.

The cubs are miniatures of the parents, they appear darker because the spots are closer together. The female normally has four pairs of teats.

Distribution

The distribution of the Leopard is extremely wide, being common in Africa South of the Sahara and still maintaining a foothold in the North of the continent. It is present in Asia Minor and is beginning to re-colonise the Sinai Peninsula and Israel. The range then extends eastwards to the Amur district of Siberia and South to the Malayan Peninsula and Indo-china. There are no reports of it occurring on the Tibetan plateau. It does not occur on the islands of Sakhalin or Sumatra but it is found in Java and Sri Lanka and may still be present in Zanzibar. There are reports of it occurring on Bali although because of the scanty nature of the reports the identification is doubtful.

The Leopard is also found on the North slopes of the Caucasus mountains which makes it a perfectly acceptable European species.

Habitat

Within their range Leopards occupy a bewildering variety of habitats, the only type of country that they shun is outright desert. They are seldom seen more than 3,000 metres above sea level and there are only two reports from above 4,000 metres. They will tolerate a little snow but probably do not overwinter at high altitudes. In areas where they have a choice of habitat they appear to favour savannah and scrubland over and above thick jungle.

Habits

Since the Leopard is a very adaptable animal it is difficult to give an accurate picture of its habits. It certainly appears to be solitary but there are confusing reports of pairs being seen together and even six adults have been seen at once. The existence of a collective noun, a 'leap' of Leopards may indicate that there are occasions when they are frequently seen together. Schaller reported that he only saw pairs of Leopards on three occasions.

Whether the Leopard is nocturnal or diurnal, in any district depends on the level of competition from other species, on the degree of persecution by Man and on the availability of prey.

They are often seen during daylight in National Parks in Africa, outside the Parks however they are nocturnal, their tracks attest to a reasonable number of animals being present. In India where the Leopard faces competition from Tigers it is a nocturnal animal but in Sri Lanka where it is the top predator it is frequently seen by daylight. In the Sinai desert the Leopard is diurnal because their only sources of food spend the night in situations where they would hear the approach of a predator.

The males hold territories which sometimes overlap those of other males, individuals space themselves out by means of marking and will visit every part of their territory every third or fourth week. Females also will hold a territory which may be within that of a male, again territories of females may overlap each other. Nomads looking for vacant territories to occupy for themselves pass through the territories of residents and appear to be tolerated. Leopards are known to travel twenty-five kilometres in a night and may on occasion travel as much as seventy-five kilometres.

The Leopard hunts its prey by stalking till it is close and then making a rush followed by a swift leap, this rush can be as fast as 60 kilometres per hour, and the leap may be up to six metres. The normal method of killing is a bite either at the throat of the prey or on the nape of the neck. The cat then usually starts by eating the viscera of the prey, frequently dragging the carcase a little distance before starting to eat. When the Leopard has finished eating it stores the remainder of the carcase in a tree, some stored carcases are quite heavy, there is an eyewitness report of a giraffe calf weighing 90 kg. being cached in a branch 3.6 metres above the ground. However in some areas, presumably those where there is little to fear from scavengers, the Leopard does not trouble to place the kill in a tree but merely contents itself with hiding it in the undergrowth.

The range of prey taken by the Leopard is extremely wide and includes fish, mice and all animals up to a bodyweight of around 90 kg., although more usually the upper limit is about 60 kg. Domestic stock and people are sometimes eaten and it is for these reasons that Leopards are shot by local inhabitants after such incidents. In Africa the Leopard and the Baboon are the principal predators on each other. Schaller found that in the Serengeti the most important prey species for the Leopard was the Thompson's Gazelle *(Gazella thomsoni)*. Wild Boar will sometimes put a charging Leopard to flight but the principal enemies of the Leopard are Lion, Tiger and Man.

Breeding

Throughout most of its range the Leopard has no fixed breeding season, but in eastern Siberia and northern China mating takes place in January and February whilst in the Caucasus the breeding season is in February and March. The female is receptive to the male for about seven days and the inter-oestrous period is about forty-seven days. The act of mating is accompanied by a large amount of snarling and growling, during copulation the male bites the neck of the female in typical cat fashion and as they break apart she turns on him with bites and snarls.

The den is made in any suitable place such as a crevice amongst rocks or even in a clump of dense grass. The male usually takes no part in the rearing of the cubs, although there is one report from the eastern Transvaal of both parents, two grown cubs from previous litters and four small cubs all sharing a cleft in a granite outcrop. Sometimes it has been observed that a male coming into the territory of a female will kill any cubs that have been sired by another male.

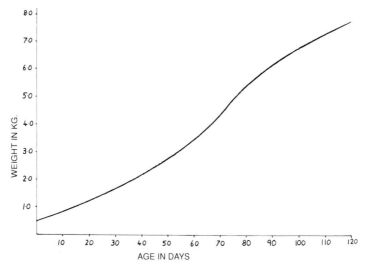

Average weight gain in Leopard Cubs

118

The composition of maternal milk is as follows:-

Water	80.6%
Fat	6.5%
Protein	11.1%
Carbohydrate	4.2%
Ash	0.75%

Development of the Young

The cubs are born blind but fully furred with fluffy downy coats that are lighter than those of the adults. The eyes open when they are about nine or ten days old. When they are about five weeks old they start to leave the den. The adult coat is gained when they are about four months old. At about ten and a half months old the deciduous teeth are lost and the permanent ones are all through. The cubs are weaned at about three months, they begin to lead separate lives between eighteen months and two years. Full adult size is reached at about three years.

Status and Systematics

Some sub-species of Leopard are getting rare because of the demand for their coats and because of the destruction of their habitats, others however are keeping their numbers up and, in areas such as the Sinai, the Leopard has recently been recorded for the first time in living memory.

There are many sub-species of Leopard, not all of which are accepted as valid by some authorities.

The International Species Indexing System numbers are as follows:-

1412007002004	Leopard File Number	
1412007002004001	*Panthera pardus*	General Entry
1412007002004002	*Panthera pardus pardus*	Sudan, Ethiopia, Congo, Kenya
1412007002004003	*Panthera pardus ciscaucasia*	Kuban, Siberia
1412007002004004	*Panthera pardus delacouri*	Indo-china
1412007002004005	*Panthera pardus fusca*	Kashmir to Sri Lanka Burma, South China
1412007002004006	*Panthera pardus japonensis*	North China
1412007002004007	*Panthera pardus jarvisi*	Sinai

1412007002004008	*Panthera pardus leopardus*	West Africa
1412007002004009	*Panthera pardus melanotica*	South Africa
1412007002004010	*Panthera pardus nimr*	Arabia
1412007002004011	*Panthera pardus orientalis*	Korea - Amur
1412007002004012	*Panthera pardus panthera*	Algeria, Egypt
1412007002004013	*Panthera pardus pernigra*	Sikkim - Nepal, Kashmir
1412007002004014	*Panthera pardus saxicolor*	North Iran, Afghanistan
1412007002004015	*Panthera pardus sindica*	Baluchistan to Sind
1412007002004016	*Panthera pardus tulliana*	Asia Minor

Additionally the following sub-species are accepted by some authorities

Panthera pardus adersi	Zanzibar Island
Panthera pardus antinorii	Eritrea
Panthera pardus ehui	Uganda
Panthera pardus dathei	Central Iran
Panthera pardus ituriensis	Congo
Panthera pardus kotiya	Sri Lanka
Panthera pardus melas	Java
Panthera pardus millardi	Kashmir
Panthera pardus nanopardus	Somalia
Panthera pardus shortridgei	Central Africa
Panthera pardus suahelica	East Africa

Chapter Thirty-six

JAGUAR
Panthera onca Linnaeus 1758

Vital Statistics

Length	head and body	male 1.2 - 1.8 metres
		female 1.14 - 1.6 metres
	tail	male 0.52 - 0.66 metres
		female 0.43 - 0.6 metres
Height at shoulder		0.68 - 0.76 metres
Weight		36 - 158 kg.
Age at maturity		approx. 2 - 3 years
Dental formula		$I\,^3/_3$ $C\,^1/_1$ $P\,^3/_2$ $M\,^1/_1$
Chromosome count		38
Karyotype		1 (Robinson)
Longevity		over 20 years
Gestation period		98 - 108 days
Number of young		1 - 4
Weight at birth		approx. 800 g.
Age weaned		approx. 22 weeks

Description

A very large heavily built cat with a powerful looking head and body, this species has a very deep chest and a rounded head. The ground colour of the coat varies from pale yellow through shades of ochre to a rusty ruddy brown, the chest, belly and insides of the limbs are whitish in colour. There are black rosettes all over the back and flanks which sometimes have black spots in their centres, along the centre of the back the rosettes give way to elongated spots which sometimes merge to form a dorsal line. The tail has black rings around it, the collar markings on the chest are usually complete and the ears have black backs with white centres. Individuals from open country are frequently lighter in colour than those from heavily forested regions.

Melanistic individuals are quite common, in some areas they are more plentiful than spotted animals, this has led some authorities to believe that the melanistic gene in Jaguars is dominant rather than recessive. Albino and partial albino specimens have also been reported especially from Paraguay.

Distribution and Habitat

The Jaguar is found in the Mexican states and from there it spreads southwards as far as northern Argentina, Paraguay and Uruguay. Formerly it was also present in the United States and central Argentina, there are even scattered reports that some individuals were found at the Straits of Magellan.

Within its range the Jaguar is found in every sort of country except outright desert, it is found down at sea level and is relatively plentiful in Bolivia, 2,700 metres up in the Andes.

Habits

With field studies only starting recently little is known of the habits of the Jaguar in the wild. Over most of its range it is considered to be nocturnal, but it has been observed that in areas where they are safe from man they become diurnal. They are far more water loving than Leopards and may often be seen swimming across rivers during their hunting expeditions.

It has been found that the territories of neighbouring females will overlap and that several females may be found within the territory of one male. Reports from travellers indicate that adult Jaguars will often be found close together. The method of marking the territory is assumed to be by scratching on trees and by spraying urine against established scent posts. In Mexico the size of the home range of males was found to be 100-190 square kilometres and in Brazil that of females 25-38 square kilometres.

For the most part Jaguars appear to be solitary except during the breeding season when adults may be encountered together. Vocalizations of the Jaguar include the 'sawing grunt' similar to that of the Leopard roaring, a low deep throated growl and a yelp like that of a Domestic Cat much magnified.

The Jaguars favourite method of killing prey is to bite straight through the skull inflicting brain damage. The prey consists mostly of mammals, which may be as large as a Tapir, in most areas the favourite prey animal is the Peccary. Box turtles are known to form part of the diet. When the cat has had its fill it will retire to a hiding place to digest the meal, returning to the carcase later to eat again. Sometimes they will drag the carcase a considerable distance before they begin to eat. They have been known to pull a horse over a kilometre and a half, passing through a small river on the way. Occasionally a Jaguar will become a man-eater, but such instances are rare.

Breeding

Over most of its range the Jaguar has no fixed breeding season but in the northerly areas mating takes place in January. This is when the largest number of Jaguars are seen together, as many as eight males have been seen courting one female. The oestrous period lasts for about eight days.

The female makes her den in close cover, in one case rocks at the foot of a waterfall were chosen, and there she gives birth to between one and four cubs. It is probable that in the wild the female will give birth every second year although there is one well authenticated case of a female giving birth two years running.

The composition of the maternal milk is as follows:-

Solids	28.2%
Fat	7.8%
Protein	13.7%
Carbohydrate	2.7%

Development of Young

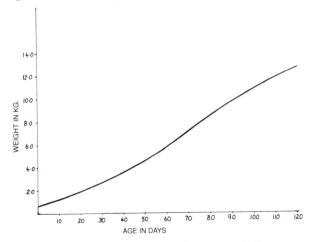

Average Weight Gain in Jaguar Cubs

Mostly the cubs are born blind with their eyes opening before the end of the first week. The deciduous teeth start to appear in about nine days, and the lower canines have erupted by about five weeks. Also by about five weeks the cubs start to climb out of the den, and may be seen playing with each other. By eleven weeks of age they are regularly eating meat and at about thirteen weeks they will guard the meat from each other. The cubs are weaned at about twenty-two weeks and become mature at about three years.

Status and Systematics

Nowhere is the Jaguar considered plentiful, in the northerly and southerly parts of its range it is being threatened by the demands of the fur trade; elsewhere it is regarded as vulnerable.

There are usually considered to be eight sub-species of Jaguar.

The International Species Indexing System numbers are as follows:-

1412007002003 Jaguar File Number

Number	Species	Range
1412007002003001	*Panthera onca*	General Entry
1412007002003002	*Panthera onca onca*	Venezuela - East Central Brazil
1412007002003003	*Panthera onca arizonensis*	Arizona, North West Mexico - Sonora
1412007002003004	*Panthera onca centralis*	Chiapas, Mexico - Colombia
1412007002003005	*Panthera onca goldmani*	Yucatan Peninsula North Guatemala
1412007002003006	*Panthera onca hernandesii*	South Sonora - Chiapas
1412007002003007	*Panthera onca palustris*	South Bolivia - Mato Grosso - Central Argentina
1412007002003008	*Panthera onca peruvianus*	Peru
1412007002003009	*Panthera onca veracrucis*	South Mexico - North Chiapas

Chapter Thirty-seven

TIGER
Panthera tigris Linnaeus 1778

Vital Statistics

Length	head and body	male 180 - 290 cm.
		female 160 - 175 cm.
	tail	male 80 - 100 cm.
		female 82 - 88 cm.
Height at shoulder		85 - 124 cm.
Weight		192 - 324 kg.
Age at Maturity		male 2 - 2½ years
		female about 3 years
Dental Formula		$I^3/_3$ $C^1/_1$ $P^3/_2$ $M^1/_1$
Chromosome count		38
Karyotype		1 (Robinson)
Longevity		up to 26 years
Gestation period		103 - 110 days
Number of young		1 - 7
Weight at birth		about 1.36 kg.
Age weaned		5 - 6 months

Description

The Tiger is the largest of all cats and has very distinct markings. The ground colour of the coat varies from pale straw yellow to tawny orange, there are dark stripes on the back and flanks of the animal which may be grey, brown or black. These stripes run laterally on the coat and it is possible to see in some of them a resemblance to much elongated spots or rosettes. The muzzle, throat, chest, belly and inside of the limbs are lighter in colour or even white, the backs of the ears are black with white centres, the tail has rings around it all along its length. The male has a deep ruff of fur around the sides of the neck.

Some Tigers have coats that are almost white together with eyes of ice blue, albinos are also reported with the characteristic pink eyes. Melanistic animals have been reported from time to time but only one of these reports has been confirmed.

The female normally has three pairs of teats.

Distribution

The Tiger is exclusively an Asiatic animal, it is found in Iran and eastwards to the Pacific, being present in Siberia as far North as the river Aldon. It is not present on the Tibetan plateau nor on the Island Sri Lanka and is rarely seen on Sakhalin Island. On the mainland it is not found in southern Iran, southern Afghanistan and Pakistan.

Habitat

The only requirements that a Tiger needs from its habitat are cover, water and sufficient prey, this means that the Tiger can be found in a vast range of different types of country including tall grass, reed thickets and all types of forest. Tigers may be found at sea level and have been seen as high as 4,000 metres above sea level.

Habits

It is difficult to convey a picture of the Tigers habits because with this species, as with the Leopard, the individuals vary so much from each other. The gait of the Tiger is similar to that of the camel, where the animal moves first the legs on the right side and then those on the left, this gives the animal a gliding sinuous walk from which it can break into a run without pause. When running Tigers are capable of making jumps of more than seven metres long.

It is very rare for adult Tigers to climb trees but juveniles will do so readily, however all Tigers will take to water both for travelling, for hunting, and just to cool off in the heat of the day. The Tiger usually lays up during the heat of the day only venturing out during the twilight hours and at night, in cooler climes and where hunting has been stopped the species has become more diurnal in its habits.

For the most part Tigers are solitary animals, however there are occasions when as many as eight individuals have been seen together, these concentrations are usually around kills, on such occasions the animals are very well behaved and only feed on the kill one at a time. Such good behaviour may be the result of an order of hierarchy among the animals although it is not known how such an arrangement is arrived at, it is however probable that the resident of the area has the first right to feed on the kill.

Tigers appear to stay within a given area for the purposes of hunting, they mark a territory but do not appear to defend it as long as other Tigers stick to the rules. Nomad Tigers will pass through the territory but generally will not stay. It appears that the territory of a male may encompass those of several females. Marking with scrapes, faeces, urine, etc., may serve as a mechanism for keeping the individuals spaced out from one another. In addition to resident Tigers there are many individuals within the population that are usually referred to as transients or nomads; mostly these are juveniles looking for a territory of their own. These nomads will sometimes interact with residents, both male and female. When passing through an occupied territory they always advertise their presence so that the resident will not get suspicious of them. The size of territory held by a Tiger varies widely with the local conditions, being as little as 65 square kilometres in some parts of India, and as much as 3,000 square kilometres in some parts of Siberia. One Tiger in the Ussuri region is known to have travelled 1,000 kilometres in three weeks looking for food. The more usual distance a Tiger will travel is 15 - 20 kilometres in twenty-four hours, and in good habitats the Siberian Tiger has a territory of 200 - 205 square kilometres.

As with other cats the range of prey taken by the Tiger is quite wide, they quite commonly kill Buffalo (*Bubalus arnee*), Gaur (*Bos gaurus*), Sambar (*Cervus unicolor*), and other animals of that size, they have even been known to kill adult Elephant (*Elephas maximus*) and Rhinoceros (*Rhinoceros unicornis*) calves. In the Primorie region Wild Boar (*Sus scrofa*) make up 52% of the diet and Elk (*Alces alces*) 37%. If nothing else is available they will eat frogs, locusts and crustaceans. Domestic animals are sometimes eaten, although studies have shown this to be the exception rather than the rule, Man-eating is very rare. The Tigers favoured method of hunting is to locate the prey by sight or sound, often waiting to ambush, then to stalk up close, using all available cover, and then to spring onto the back. If the prey is too big it is grasped by the throat and suffocated. Very big animals may be hamstrung before being killed. The Tiger will return to the carcase to eat several times until it is finished, sometimes the prey is dragged a long distance and concealed before eating starts, even heavy animals such as horses have been dragged 500 metres.

The Tiger has a range of vocalisations comprising, purring, prusten, pooking, grunting, mewing, woofing, moaning and roaring. Some of these calls are used to advertise the presence of the animal and some are used when in contact with other individuals, roaring and moaning can also serve as threat calls.

Breeding

In captivity and in warmer climes Tigers do not appear to have a fixed breeding season, in Siberia however they are definitely seasonal breeders. The peak of births occurs in the Springtime, with oestrous activity spread out over a three to four month period, whilst for eight months many females go into anoestrus. Normally the oestrous period lasts for ten to fifteen days, while the inter-oestrous period is extremely variable it appears to average about seven weeks. Oestrous is usually accompanied by much roaring and head rubbing before mating takes place, often males will fight for a female frequently inflicting deep cuts and scratches on each other, these fights however never end in death. Unlike the Lion the female throws the male off after copulation and actually attacks him. Mating happens many times a day.

The female makes her den in any convenient close cover, this may be among rocks, in a cave, or occasionally in a hollow tree or a thicket. The male takes no part in the upbringing of the cubs.

The composition of the maternal milk is as follows:-

Solids	24.4%
Fat	8.4%
Protein	10.5%
Carbohydrate	3%

Development of Young

The cubs are born blind but fully furred, their eyes open between nine and twelve days after birth. When they are twelve days old they can clutch with their claws and lick themselves. At about fourteen days they respond to the mothers voice and crawl around. By the time that they are about three weeks old they are able to walk on all fours. Also at about three weeks old the deciduous teeth start to appear, the permanent teeth do not start to appear until about ten months of age. The cubs suckle for up to six months, during which time the mother will move them from den to den for greater protection. The mother teaches the cubs how to hunt during the ensuing months, and they become independent at about eighteen months. By the time that they are three years old they are fully mature.

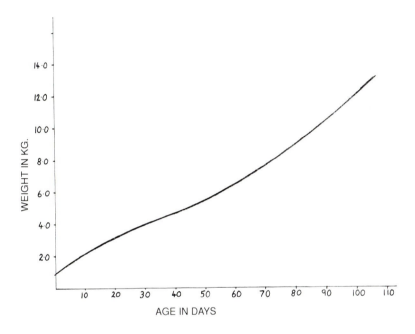

Average weight gain in Tiger Cubs

Status and Systematics

Most sub-species of the Tiger are endangered and some of them may already be extinct, the principal pressure comes from deforestation, the fur trade and trophy hunting; shooting of rogue animals that kill domestic stock and Man accounts for very few individuals.

In 1984-85 a census of Tigers in the Primorie region of Siberia revealed a population of between 283 and 293 animals.

Some authorities recognise seven sub-species, some eight, and some nine.

The International Species Indexing System numbers are as follows:-

1412007002005	Tiger File Number	
1412007002005001	*Panthera tigris*	General Entry
1412007002005002	*Panthera tigris tigris*	India
1412007002005003	*Panthera tigris altaica*	East Siberia, Korea, Manchuria
1412007002005004	*Panthera tigris amoyensis*	South China
1412007002005005	*Panthera tigris corbetti*	South China, Indochina
1412007002005006	*Panthera tigris sondaica*	Java
1412007002005007	*Panthera tigris sumatrae*	Sumatra
1412007002005008	*Panthera tigris virgata*	Transcaucasia

The following sub-species are also recognised by some authorities:-

Panthera tigris balica	Bali
Panthera tigris lecoqui	Lop Nor region

Chapter Thirty-eight

LION
Panthera leo Linnaeus 1758

Vital Statistics

Length	head and body	male 1.70 - 1.90 metres
		female 1.40 - 1.75 metres
	tail	male 0.90 - 1.05 metres
		female 0.70 - 1.00 metres
Height at shoulder		0.80 - 1.10 metres
Weight		male 148 - 375 kg.
		female 120 - 185 kg.
Age at maturity		2 - 2½ years
Dental formula		$I^3/_3$ $C^1/_1$ $P^3/_2$ $M^1/_1$
Chromosome count		38
Karyotype		1 (Robinson)
Longevity		up to 29 years
Gestation period		103 - 119 days
Number of young		1 - 7
Weight at birth		1.10 - 1.37 kg.
Age weaned		approx. 6 months

Description

A very large cat with a broad face and rounded ears, the body is very muscular with a fairly squat neck. The coat colour varies from a light sandy yellow through various shades to a deep ochre which is almost tawny. The underside of the belly and the inside of the legs are lighter in colour; the backs of the ears have black patches and there is a prominent black tuft at the end of the tail. This tuft conceals a horny spur which is found only on this species. The cubs have a spotted coat which they usually lose at about the age of six months, however some cubs have been born without spots and it has also been known for some individuals to keep their spots for all of their lives. The male has a large mane composed of long hair around the head, neck, shoulders and chest, the main is usually darker in colour than the coat and in some instances may be black. The mane tends to grow darker as the Lion grows older. From time to time albino individuals have been seen. Melanistic specimens are not known although some animals have been seen who have very large black patches on their coats.

131

The eyes are unusual in that they have a band across the centre of the eye which gives greater magnification than the areas above and below, they are a bit like bifocal lenses on human spectacles.

The females usually have two pairs of teats, although some individuals have been recorded with three pairs.

Distribution

In historic times the Lion was found in Europe as far West as Greece, from there it ranged throughout the Middle East to India and was found throughout all of Africa. Today the range is limited to the Gir forest in India and to Africa South of the Sahara. The last wild Lions in North Africa and Iran were recorded in the 1920's. In South Africa today no Lions are found South of the Orange river. For a long time they were absent from Natal but in the early 1960's a pair established themselves in the Umfolozi reserve, their fate is not recorded.

Habitat

The Lion will tolerate a fairly wide spectrum of territorial types, but its undoubted preference is for grassland and lightly wooded scrub. Sometimes Lions will penetrate semi-desert but they will usually stay out of dense forest. They have been reported entering rain forest in Uganda after the wet season and they also frequent the bamboo forest of the Virunga Volcanoes. They are found everywhere from sea-level to 5,000 metres, close to the snow line on African mountains.

Habits

The Lion is the most diurnal of all cats and is also the most gregarious, their ordinary life is spent living in groups known as 'prides'. The pride consists of a number of females who inhabit a tract of land, the land is defended by two or three males who also father the offspring of the females. The males may remain with the pride for two or three years after which time they are usually ousted by younger males. The males who are driven out either find other prides or join the numbers of nomads who have no fixed pride, occasionally they may regain the pride that they were driven from. More usually they finish their days as nomads. It is the males who mark the territory of the pride and defend it against intruding males . A pride that loses its males has little hope of surviving unless a new male or males take over.

The females are permanent members of the pride and it is they who do the hunting, frequently they work as a team with some females driving the prey towards others. Although it is the females who do the killing it is the male who takes first share of the kill, females and cubs must wait until the males have finished. The prey of the Lion consists mostly of large antelope although Giraffe, Buffalo and Wart-hogs are also taken. Fairly large prey is preferred because it will feed the whole pride. When food is scarce Lions will also kill cane-rats, gerbils, quails, snakes, crocodiles, tortoises, fish, locusts, and termites. Also Lions do not refuse carrion, fruit, peanuts, grass and garbage from African villages. At the other end of the scale Lions have been known to kill Elephant calves, Rhinoceros and Hippopotamus. It is abundantly clear that a Lion will eat anything that is edible including Lion cubs.

Most of the Lion's hunting is done in the cool of the evening, however Lions will move about just as well after dark as they do by daylight, the middle part of the day is usually occupied sleeping. The Lion is almost exclusively terrestrial, just occasionally they will climb trees to locate prey. When the prey is located by sight the Lionesses often hunt as a team using a pincer movement singling out the prey from the herd. Sometimes the prey is eaten on the spot and sometimes dragged away to cover, when the pride is a small one the remains of the carcase are often covered in order to be finished later, kills made in the daytime are often finished by vultures. Sometimes Lions will steal the kills of other predators such as Hunting Dogs or Hyenas.

The vocalizations of the Lion are as varied as those of the other cats, the characteristic roaring is used to communicate with other members of the pride and also to proclaim the territory to possible intruders. Growling, snorts, hisses and whimpering have all been heard from Lions, they have even been known to purr although they cannot do this continuously.

There are many young adult individuals in the population who have been driven out of prides because the territory of the pride was unable to support them. These individuals are known as nomads, and they are forced to live a life on the move unless they can attach themselves to a pride. Nomads are of both sexes, although there is a higher proportion of males. Nomads have been seen to share a kill with a pride and have sometimes banded together to try and form a pride where local conditions permit. Since these associations usually form in fringe areas during the rainy season they rarely persist all year. There is a case of an entire litter of sub-adult females staying together after leaving the maternal pride and forming a permanent pride of their own.

The number of Lions in a pride varies enormously with the local conditions, though in favourable circumstances there may be as many as thirty-five animals in permanent association with each other. The maximum age of pride males in the Kruger National Park was found to be ten to eleven years, and the maximum age of females fourteen to fifteen years. In the Nairobi National Park one female still with a pride was known to be twenty-two years old. Many Lions are killed by disease or parasites, which includes tapeworm, trypanosomes and ticks. Some Lions are killed by other Lions and some by other animals such as Gemsbok, Buffalo, Elephant, Zebra and poachers. Lions are also incapacitated by wounds from fights and porcupine quills. Wounded and elderly Lions are not necessarily doomed since there are records of young Lions and Lionesses doing all the hunting for themselves and for an elderly companion.

Breeding

In the wild there does not appear to be a fixed breeding season, this also applies in captivity. The female comes into oestrous for between four and fourteen days, the inter-oestrous period averages five weeks. Females in the wild appear to have their first oestrous at three and a half years of age, in captivity the first oestrous has been observed at two years old. Males in the wild appear to mate for the first time at three and a half to four years of age, although in captivity this has been observed to happen at two and a half years of age.

All mating is the preserve of the pride males who monopolise the females, driving off all intruding males. When they take over a pride males will frequently kill any small cubs who may be there in order that all offspring will be their own. Some females appear to breed until they die of old age whilst others reach the limit of their breeding at about fifteen years. The female leaves the vicinity of the pride in order to have her cubs in the seclusion of her own lair, she will rejoin the pride after about three weeks or alternatively in exceptional circumstances will bring up the cubs herself. If the cubs die for any reason she may come into oestrous as little as seven days later. The Lioness will not normally mate again until the cubs are eighteen months to two years old, although there is a report of a female conceiving when her previous offspring were fifteen months old.

The composition of the maternal milk is as follows:-

Solids	30.2%
Fat	17.5%
Protein	9.3%
Carbohydrate	3.4%

Development of Young

Usually Lion cubs are born blind, but just occasionally they are born with their eyes open. They remain in the lair until they are able to walk, although the mother will often transfer them from one hiding place to another. They are usually able to walk by about the fourth or fifth week. They will suckle until they are about five or six months old; whilst with the pride they will suckle not only from their own mother but also from any other Lioness who is lactating.

The incisor teeth begin to erupt at about three weeks of age and the deciduous teeth are replaced by permanent ones at about one year old. At around four or five weeks play behaviour commences including mock stalking and pouncing. Also, at this time they start eating meat. In captivity Lionesses have been seen to disgorge partially digested meat for the cubs, it is probable that this happens in the wild as well. Cubs will start to follow hunting parties when they are about seven months old. When males are about one year old the mane starts to appear.

Whilst the cubs are with the pride they are tolerated by the adult males, however they find it very difficult to get a share of meat at a kill and many cubs die from this and a variety of other causes. At the end of the first year the survival rate is around 50%.

When they are two to three years old males are forced out of the pride to become nomads, often females are also forced out, sometimes they will stay together forming a juvenile group.

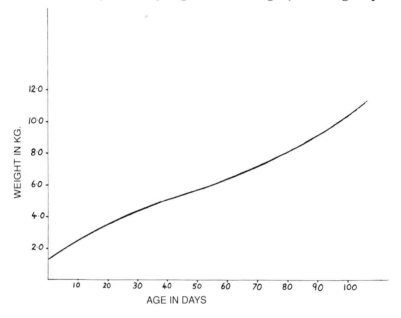

Average weight gain in Lion Cubs

Status and Systematics

In India the Lion is vulnerable because the very small area it inhabits makes it vulnerable to pressures from domestic stock being grazed within the boundaries of the reserve.

In Africa some races are thriving and some are on the brink of extinction.

There are generally considered to be eleven subspecies.

The International Species Indexing System numbers are as follows:-

1412007002001	Lion File Number	
1412007002001001	*Panthera leo*	General Entry
1412007002001002	*Panthera leo leo*	North Africa
1412007002001003	*Panthera leo azandica*	Congo
1412007002001004	*Panthera leo bleyenberghi*	Angola, Zimbabwe
1412007002001005	*Panthera leo hollisteri*	Congo
1412007002001006	*Panthera leo massaicus*	Uganda, Kenya
1412007002001007	*Panthera leo melanochaita*	Cape Province
1412007002001008	*Panthera leo persica*	Gir forest, India
1412007002001009	*Panthera leo roosevelti*	Sudan, Ethiopia
1412007002001010	*Panthera leo senegalensis*	Senegal - Cameroon
1412007002001011	*Panthera leo somaliensis*	Somalia
1412007002001012	*Panthera leo verneyi*	South West Africa

Additionally some authorities also recognise the following two subspecies:-

Panthera leo goojeratensis	India (leaving *P.l. persica* for Iran & Afghanistan)
Panthera leo krugeri	Kruger National Park

Chapter Thirty-nine

CHEETAH
Acinonyx jubatus Schreber 1776

Vital Statistics

Length	head and body	1.20 - 1.52 metres
	tail	0.65 - 0.85 metres
Height at shoulder		0.74 - 0.90 metres
Weight		30 - 63 kg.
Dental formula		$I\,^3/_3$ $C\,^1/_1$ $P\,^3/_2$ $M\,^1/_1$
Chromosome count		38
Karyotype		2 (Robinson)
Longevity		up to 17 years
Gestation period		approx. 92 days
Number of young		1 - 8
Weight at birth		approx. 270 g.
Age weaned		47 months

Description

A large cat, very slender about the stomach and having a deep chest, a small head, long legs and a slender tail. The ground colour of the coat varies from a pale gold colour through various shades of ochre till it is almost a tawny brown, the underneath of the throat, chest, stomach and the inside of the limbs are paler in colour, in some cases white. There are black stripes from the inner corners of the eyes to the mouth and there are black spots scattered all over the coat, these spots are less well defined on the undersides. The tail is spotted for part of its length and is ringed with black for the final third finishing with a bushy tip which is white underneath. The ears are small and have the backs ringed with black, being greyish in the centre.

Both melanistic and albinistic specimens have been recorded and in the Kruger National Park and at the De Witt Centre there are numerous records of individuals which have longitudinal black stripes. These were formerly regarded as a separate species, the 'King Cheetah', research has now shown these individuals colouration to be due to a mutant form of the 'tabby' gene.

The cubs have long woolly capes which are pale grey in colour, these they gradually lose , although some males retain the remnants of the cape in the form of a rudimentary mane.

There is no gap between the canine and premolar teeth, this results in the muzzle looking curiously short in comparison with other cats. The hyoid is completely bone (making the Cheetah technically a small cat) and the pupils of the eyes are round. Adults are unable to retract their claws, observations on cubs born in captivity have produced disagreement as to whether or not they can retract their claws during the first four months of life.

The eyes have a broad horizontal band across the centre which magnifies the vision in that region compared with the view above and below this area, rather like bifocal spectacles.

The female normally has six pairs of teats.

Distribution

The Cheetah was formerly found throughout Africa and the Middle East and as far away as India. In the present day only a remnant population is left in North Africa. South of the Sahara it remains present in fair numbers everywhere except in dense rain forest and much of the Republic of South Africa. There have been no recorded sightings in Arabia since 1950 and the Indian Cheetah was declared extinct in 1952, recent observations however indicate that this sub-species may still survive. Before the revolution in Iran there were known to be at least three hundred Cheetahs present in that country, news of their fate in recent years has not become generally available.

Habitat

Although the Cheetah is generally assumed to be an animal of the open grasslands and sparse woodland, there is evidence emerging that it will on occasions also frequent dense woodland. In South West Africa the Cheetah is also found on stony ridges and in the sand veldt, throughout much of their range they will also use the thornbush along the river valleys.

Habits

The Cheetah is largely a terrestrial animal although it will use trees as lookouts to locate prey and as an ambush point.

Since Cheetahs hunt by sight they are primarily diurnal, the Cheetah's method of hunting is to stalk the prey until it is close and then to make a fast and furious rush in the course of which it may reach a speed of 114 kilometres per hour. When it is close enough the Cheetah will knock the animal over and then go for the throat, strangling the quarry. Field studies have revealed that the Cheetah is successful in as many as 50% of the attempts that it makes to kill.

There is a case on record where a Cheetah and Jackal co-operated in hunting.

For the most part Cheetahs are solitary animals but there are occasions on which they form groups, the size of the groups varies widely and usually consists of litters and their parents. On occasions when adults associate they are frequently litter mates who have not yet gone their separate ways. With non related adults males will more often form groups than females, when they do so adult males usually travel in pairs but one group of four stayed together in Nairobi National Park for two years.

Cheetah do not appear to defend a territory, the area that they use varies from fifty to one hundred and thirty square kilometres. There are however reports of three males killing another male who wandered into the area they were occupying. The area occupied is not exclusive to one individual or group but overlaps to a large degree the hunting range of others. Cheetahs seem to work on a policy of mutual avoidance which they operate by use of scent marking. Other Cheetah will smell the scent and if it is fresh they will usually move off in a different direction from that taken by the animal who did the marking. If they do come into a confrontation with each other they make use of a threat display in which they keep their heads low, raise their hindquarters and make stiff legged short bounding movements forward at each other.

The range of prey taken by the Cheetah consists of anything from rodents up to animals the size of Kongoni and Waterbuck, the preferred prey animals are Gazelles and Impala, more rarely Warthog, Giraffe, Aardvark and Porcupine are taken. Sometimes the Cheetah is driven off by the prey. Often other predators will take the prey off the Cheetah, sometimes Cheetah will even scavenge, these are indications that the Cheetah is low in the predator hierarchy.

The vocalizations of the Cheetah are different from those of other cats, females in oestrous give a yelping call which appears designed to attract males, this call is frequently associated with submission. Another call made by the female in oestrous is the stutter call, although females making this call are usually aggressive towards the male. The most frequently heard call is the chirrup, this is used in many situations, it is used between mother and cubs, and also between males and females. Growls and spitting are also emitted on occasions.

Breeding

There does not appear to be a fixed breeding season either in the wild or in captivity. The oestrous period varies from four to fourteen days during which time the female may be courted by several males. Captive females have been known to mate with more than one male but it is not known if this happens in the wild. The gestation period has been found by observation in captivity to be ninety to ninety-five days and the size of the litter from one to eight, the most usual numbers being four or five. If the litter fails to survive the female will come into oestrous after about ten days.

The female gives birth in a nest which she makes in a thornbush or tall dense grass, whilst the cubs are with her she moves her location every two or three days covering her whole range in about ten days. The male takes no part in the upbringing of the cubs.

The composition of the maternal milk is as follows:-

Solids	23.2%
Fat	9.5%
Protein	9.4%
Carbohydrate	3.5%

Development of Young

The cubs are born with their eyes closed, generally the eyes open by about the fifth day and are able to focus fully by about the ninth day. During the second week they commence crawl-

141

ing and by the end of the third week are able to stand on all fours, it is about this time that the deciduous teeth start to appear and play between the youngsters begins. The characteristic mane of the young Cheetah starts to grow at around three weeks, also at this time they start climbing, an ability they largely lose later, it is at this time that they can retract their claws. At four weeks they will defend themselves by lashing out with their claws, they will then begin eating solid meat. They continue suckling however for between five and seven months. After they are three months old their mother introduces them to live prey.

They will lose their mane towards the end of the first year and they become independent at about fifteen to eighteen months. Males frequently stay together for some time before settling into an area of their own, females tend to leave the litter group within a fairly short space of time. About half the cubs born alive die within their first eight months of life and about one third survive to be a year old.

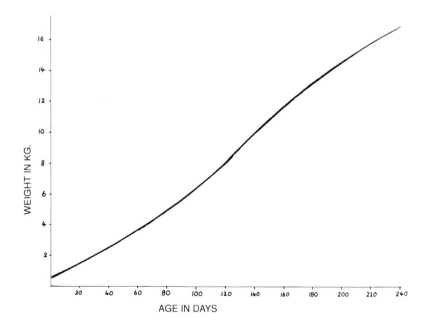

Average weight gain in Cheetah Cubs

142

Status and Systematics

The Cheetah is a threatened species throughout its range although in South Africa steps have been taken to increase the numbers through captive breeding with the intention of returning individuals to the wild. The decline in numbers of the Cheetah parallels the decline in wildlife generally in the face of increased agricultural activity. In Iran the Cheetah was increasing in numbers before the overthrow of the Shah but there is no word available on its present status.

There are commonly considered to be six sub-species, the King Cheetah is now known to be a colour variation.

The International Species Indexing System Numbers are as follows:-

1412007003001	Cheetah File Number	
1412007003001001	*Acinonyx jubatus*	General Entry
1412007003001002	*Acinonyx jubatus jubatus*	Southern Africa
1412007003001003	*Acinonyx jubatus hecki*	North Africa to Dahomey
1412007003001004	*Acinonyx jubatus ngorongorensis*	Tanzania Congo
1412007003001005	*Acinonyx jubatus raineyi*	Kenya
1412007003001006	*Acinonyx jubatus soemmeringii*	Nigeria to Somalia
1412007003001007	*Acinonyx jubatus venaticus*	Southern Asia

Chapter Forty

ONZA

This cat is not fully accepted in scientific circles yet, but its existence has been demonstrated by specimens. The following details have been gleaned from the dissection of one four year old female carried out in Mexico in 1986.

Vital Statistics

Length	head and body	113 cm.
	tail	73 cm.
Weight		27 kg.
Dental formula	$I \frac{3}{3}$ $C \frac{1}{1}$ $P \frac{3 \text{ or } 2}{2}$ $M \frac{1}{1}$	

Description

The colouration is the same as the Pumas' except that there are horizontal stripes visible on the inside of the forelimbs. Two of the four known skulls which have been examined were found to have one premolar tooth missing, in all the skulls the post canine gap was very small and the carnassials narrow.

The body is much more slender than that of the Puma and the legs, whilst longer, have much more sturdy bones. The claws are non-retractile which would seem to indicate a cursorial method of hunting like the Cheetah. The paws are narrower and more elongated than those of the Puma.

Distribution and Habitat

So far as is known the Onza is confined to the Sierra Madre Occidentale mountain range in Sonora and Sinaloa province in Mexico, occasionally descending to the lowlands. The vegetation is sub-tropical scrub in the lowlands and sub-tropical to semi-arid on the higher ground where the Onza spends most of its time. The nature of the country is such that vehicles cannot be used, and even horses find many places difficult.

Habits

Almost nothing is known of the habits of this cat, what can be said is that it eats deer, probably like other cats it will eat a broad range of species. It is said to be faster and more aggressive than either the Puma or the Jaguar. There was some indication that the dissected female had been in a fight with a Jaguar.

The local Mexicans are more afraid of the Onza than they are either of the Puma or the Jaguar. In the eighteenth century there were reports of the Onza attacking humans and even eating one.

Status and Systematics

Nothing is known about the status of this cat, and the systematics have yet to be determined.

REFERENCES AND FURTHER READING

A

Anderson, D. 1977. Gestation period of Geoffroy's Cat bred at Memphis Zoo. **International Zoo Yearbook 17:** 164 - 166.

Anon. 1976. Canada Lynx. **Dinny's Digest.**

Anon. 1983. The Clouded Leopard. **Dinny's Digest.**

Anon. 1976. A foraging display for Sand Cats. **Brookfield Bison.**

Anon. 1976. Putting the zoo back into the wild. **Brookfield Bison.**

Armstrong, J. 1977. Hand rearing of Black-footed Cats *Felis nigripes*, at the National Zoological Park, Washington. **International Zoo Yearbook 15:** 245 - 249.

Armstrong, J. 1977. The development and hand-rearing of Black-footed Cats. **'The World's Cats' Vol. 3** No.3.

Ashton, D.G. and Jones, D.M. 1980. Veterinary aspects of the management of non-domestic cats. In Barzdo, J. (Ed.), **Proceedings of ABWAK Symposium 4.** ABWAK, Bristol.

B

Badino, G. 1975. **The Big Cats.** Orbis Publishing Ltd. London.

Barnes, R.G. 1977. Breeding and hand-rearing of the Marbled Cat, *Felis marmorata*, at Los Angeles Zoo. **International Zoo Yearbook 16:** 205 - 208.

Baudy, R.E. 1971. Notes on breeding felids at the Rare Feline Breeding Centre. **International Zoo Yearbook 11:** 121 - 123.

Benzon, T.A. and Smith, R.F. 1974 Male dominance hierarchies and their possible effects on breeding in Cheetahs. **International Zoo Year Book 14:** 174 - 179.

Benzon, T.A. and Smith, R.F. 1975. A case of programmed cheetah *Acinonyx jubatus* breeding. **International Zoo Year Book 15:** 154 - 157.

Benzon, T.A. and Smith, R.F. 1977. A technique for propagating Cheetahs. **'The World's Cats' Vol.3** No. 3.

Berrie, P.M. 1978. Home range of a young female Geoffroy's Cat in Paraguay. **Carnivore Vol. 1** No. 1.

Bertram, B.C. 1975. Social factors influencing reproduction in wild Lions. **Journal of Zoology 177:** 463 - 482.

Birkenheimer, E.E. 1971 Hand-rearing the Leopard Cat **International Zoo Yearbook 11:** 118 - 121.

Blumenberg, B. 1978. Feral cats in Australia and their inclusion in the Aboriginal diet. **Carnivore Vol.1** No.1.

Bogue, G. and Ferrari, M. 1978. The predatory training of captive reared pumas. **'The World's Cats' Vol. 3** No.1.

Borner, M. 1978. Status and conservation of the Sumatran Tiger. **Carnivore Vol.1.** No.1.

Burger, M. 1966. Breeding the European Lynx at Magdeburg Zoo. **International Zoo Yearbook 6:** 182 - 183.

Burney, D. and Burney, L. 1979. Cheetah and Man. **SWARA Vol.2.** No.2.

Burton, R. 1979. **Carnivores of Europe.** Batsford Books.

C

Cabrera, M.V. 1966. Tooth trimming in two vicious Lions. **International Zoo Yearbook 5:** 192 - 193

Cade, C.E. 1969. A note on breeding the Caracal Lynx at Nairobi Zoo. **International Zoo Yearbook 8:** 45

Calvin, L.O. 1970. A brief note on the birth of Snow Leopards at Dallas Zoo. **International Zoo Yearbook 9:** 96

Chubykino, N.L. and Shilo, R.A. 1981. A study of diurnal activity rhythms in Snow Leopards at Novosibirsk Zoo. **International Zoo Yearbook 21:** 193 - 196

Cline, K.F. 1967. Diet for Siberian Tigers at Detroit Zoo. **International Zoo Yearbook 6:** 74 - 76

Cociu, M. et al. 1974. Adaptational gastro-enteritis in Siberian Tigers at Bucharest Zoo. **International Zoo Yearbook 14:** 171 - 174

Colby, E.D. 1974. Artificially induced oestrus in wild and domestic cats. **'The World's Cats', Vol. 2**

Collier, G. et al. 1978. Optimization of time and energy constraints in the feeding behaviour of cats. **Carnivore Vol.1 No.1.**

Crandall, L. 1964. **Management of wild mammals in captivity.** University of Chicago Press, Chicago.

D

Dathe, H. 1969. Breeding the Indian Leopard Cat at East Berlin Zoo. **International Zoo Yearbook 8:** 42 - 44.

Davydov, E.S. and Ordzhonikidze, S.V., 1989. Breeding Pallas Cats *(Felis manul)* at the Moscow Zoo. in **'Achievements of zoos in breeding rare and endangered species of animals',** Moscow.

De-Carvalho, C.T. 1969. Comparative growth rates of hand-reared big cats. **International Zoo News 8:** 56 - 59.

Dewar, P.P. 1978. The status and management of the Puma in British Columbia. **'The World's Cats' Vol.3.** No.1.

Dobroruka, L.J. 1969. A note on the gestation and rearing in the young of the Leopard at Prague Zoo. **International Zoo Yearbook 8:**

Dorst, J. and Dandelot, P. 1972. **A Field Guide to the Larger Mammals of Africa.** Collins, London.

Dunn, G.L., 1974. Use of a domestic cat as a foster mother for an Ocelot. **International Zoo Yearbook 14:** 218 - 219.

E

Eaton, R.L. 1970. A note on reproduction of the Cheetah. **International Zoo Yearbook 10:** 86 - 89.

Eaton, R.L. 1971. Reproductive biology and preliminary observations on mating preferences in a captive Lion. **International Zoo Yearbook 11:** 198 - 202.

Eaton, R.L. 1974. The biology and social behaviour of reproduction in the Lion. **The World's Cats' Vol.2.**

Eaton, R.L. 1974. **The Cheetah.** Krieger Publishing.

Eaton, R.L. 1977. Breeding biology of the Leopard. **Der Zoologischer Garten.**

Eaton, R.L. 1977. Breeding biology and propagation of the Ocelot *(Leopardus pardalis).* **Der Zoologischer Garten.**

Eaton, R.L. 1978. The conservation of the Leopard in Africa: Towards an authentic philosophy of conservation. **Carnivore Vol.1** No. 3.

Eaton, R.L. 1978. Interference competition amongst carnivores: A model for the evolution of social behaviour. **Carnivore Vol.2** No.1.

Eaton, R.L. 1978. Why some Felids copulate so much, a model for the evolution of copulation frequency. **Carnivore Vol.1** No.1.

Eaton, R.L. 1979. Evolution of sociality in the Felidae. **Carnivore Vol.2** No.2

Eaton, R.L. and York, W. 1970. The Lion country safari and its role in conservation, education and research. **International Zoo Yearbook, 10:** 171 - 172

Eaton, R.L. and Velander, K.A. 1977. Reproduction in the Puma: Biology, Behaviour and Ontogeny. **'The World's Cats' Vol.3** No.3

Eaton, R.L., Shorey, D.W. and Yost, R. 1978. The birth and development of Cheetahs in a wild animal park. **Der Zoologischer Garten.**

Encke, W. 1962. Birth and Breeding of Cheetahs at Krefeld Zoo. **International Zoo Yearbook 2:** 85 - 86.

Ewer, R.F. 1973. **The Carnivores.** Weidenfield and Nicholson, London.

Ewer, R.F. 1974. Vivverid behaviour and the evolution of reproductive behaviour of the Felidae. **'The World's Cats' Vol.2.**

Ewing, M. 1984. **Diets for the hand-rearing of Felidae.** Texas.

F

Fagen, R.M., and Wiley, K.S. 1978. Felid paedomorphosis with special reference to Leopardus. **Carnivore Vol.1** No. 2.

Fellner, K. Natural rearing of Clouded Leopards at Frankfurt Zoo. **International Zoo Yearbook 5:** 57 - 58.

Fitch, H., Millard, S. and Tenaza. Cheetahs. **Zoonooz.**

Florio, P.L., and Spinelli, L. 1967. Successful breeding of a Cheetah in a private zoo. **International Zoo Yearbook 7:** 150 - 152.

Florio, P.L., and Spinelli, L. 1968. A second successful breeding of Cheetahs in a private zoo. **International Zoo Yearbook 8:** 76 - 78.

Fontaine, P.A. 1964. Breeding Clouded Leopards at Dallas Zoo. **International Zoo Yearbook 5:** 57 - 58.

Foster, J.W. 1977. The induction of oestrous in the Cheetah. **'The World's Cats' Vol.3** No.3.

Fowler, M. 1977. Preventative vaccination programmes for captive wild Felids. **'The World's Cats' Vol.3** No.3.

Freeman, H.E. 1975. A Preliminary study of the behaviour of captive Snow Leopards. **International Zoo Yearbook 15:** 217 - 222.

Freeman, H.E. 1977. Breeding and behaviour of the Snow Leopard. **'The World's Cats' Vol.3** No.3.

Freeman, H.E., and Braden, K. 1977. Zoo location as a factor in the reproductive behaviour of captive Snow Leopards. **Der Zoologischer Garten.**

Freeman, H.E. and Hutchins, M. 1978. Captive management of Snow Leopards. **Der Zoologischer Garten.**

Freeman, H.E., and Hutchins, M. 1980. Captive management of Snow Leopards: II. **Der Zoologischer Garten.**

Frese, R. 1980. Some notes on breeding the Leopard Cat at West Berlin Zoo. **International Zoo Yearbook 20:** 220 - 223.

Frueh, R.J. 1968. A note on breeding Snow Leopards at St. Louis Zoo. **International Zoo Yearbook 8:** 74 - 75.

G

Gandini, G. and Baldwin, P.J., 1978. An encounter between Chimpanzees and a Leopard in Senegal. **Carnivore Vol.1** No.1.

Gandros, R. and Encke, W. 1966. Case histories of a breeding group of Cheetahs at Krefeld Zoo. **International Zoo Yearbook 6:** 275 - 276.

Garcia, J. 1975. Clouded Leopard. **San Antonia news from the zoo.**

Geidel, B. and Gensch, W. 1976. The rearing of a Clouded Leopard in the presence of the male. **International Zoo Yearbook 16:** 124 - 126.

Graebner, P. 1976. The Silent Leopard. **Dinny's Digest.**

Graham-Jones, O. 1962. Operation of Lens extraction on a Tiger. **International Zoo Yearbook 3:** 107 - 110.

Greed, R.E. 1964. White Tigers at Bristol Zoo. **International Zoo Yearbook 5:** 145 - 146.

Greenwell, J.R. 1986. Onza specimen obtained - identity being studied. **The International Society of Cryptozoology Newsletter Vol.5** No.1 p.1 - 7.

Greenwell, J.R. 1990. Personal communication on the Onza.

Grittinger, T.F. 1977. Effects of conspecific scent marking among captive male Cheetahs. **'The World's Cats' Vol.3** No. 3.

Grittinger, T.F., and Ives, J.R. 1979. Scent marking sequences in captive Cheetahs. **Carnivore Vol.2** No. 4.

Grittinger, T.F., and Konrath, R.J. 1981. Management of Snow Leopards at Milwaukee. **International Zoo News.**

Guggisberg, C.A.W., 1975. **Wild Cats of the World.** David and Charles, Newton Abbot.

H

Hall, H.F. and Pelton, M.R. 1979. Abundance, distribution and biological characteristics of free-roaming house cats in Northern Tennessee. **Carnivore Vol.2** No.2.

Hanby, J. and Bygott, D. 1983. **Lions Share.** Collins, London.

Hancock, D. and Hancock, L. Cat of many names. **Animal Kingdom Vol.74** No.1.

Hemmer, H. 1977. Biology and breeding of the Sand Cat. **'The World's Cats' Vol.3** No. 3.

Hemmer, H. 1978. The evolutionary systematics of the living Felidae, present status and current problems. **Carnivore Vol.1** No. 1 71 - 79.

Hemmer, H. 1978. Fossil history of the living Felidae. **Carnivore Vol.1** No.1.

Hemmer, H. 1979. Gestation period and post-natal development in the felids. **Carnivore Vol.2** No.2.

Henderson, G.N., and Coffey, D.J. 1980. **The International Encyclopedia of Cats.** Peerage Books, Godalming.

Herbison-Frame, G.W., and Herbison-Frame, L. 1980. Cheetahs: In a race for survival. **National Geographic.**

Hoff, W. 1961. Hand-raising baby cats at Lincoln Park Zoo, Chicago. **International Zoo Yearbook 2:** 86 - 89.

Hornocker, M.G. and Wiles, W.V. 1972. Immobilising Pumas with Phencyclidine hydrochloride. **International Zoo Yearbook 12:** 220 - 222.

Hulley, J.T. 1976. Maintenance and breeding of captive Jaguarondis at Chester Zoo and Toronto. **International Zoo Yearbook 16:** 120 - 121.

Husain, D. 1966. Breeding and rearing White Tiger, *Panthera tigris*, cubs at Delhi Zoo. **International Zoo Yearbook 6:** 187 - 192.

I

Imaizumi, Y. 1967. A new genus and species of cat from Iriomote, Ryukyu islands. **Journal of Mammalogical Society of Japan.**

Imaizumi, Y. and Takara, T. 1967. External and cranial characters of new born young of the Iriomote wild cat. **Animals and zoo.**

J

Jackman, B. and Scott, J. 1982. **The Marsh Lions.** Elm Tree Books, London.

Jayewardine, E.D.W. 1975. Breeding the Fishing Cat *Felis viverrina* in captivity. **International Zoo Yearbook 15:** 150 - 152.

Jones, M.L. 1977 Record keeping and longevity of Felids in captivity. **'The World's Cats' Vol.3** No. 3.

Joshua, J.O. 1979 **Cat Owners Encyclopedia of Veterinary Medicine.** Tropical Fish Hobbyist Books, Reigate.

K

Kachuba, M. 1977. Sexual behaviour and reproduction in Geoffroy's Cat. **Der Zoologischer Garten.**

Kitchener, S.L., Merritt, D.A., and Rosenthal, M.A. 1975. Observations on the breeding and husbandry of Snow Leopards *Panthera uncia* at Lincoln Park Zoo, Chicago. **International Zoo Yearbook 15:** 212 - 217.

Kleiman, D.G. 1974. The oestrous cycle in the Tiger. **'The World's Cats' Vol.2.**

Koford, C. 1978 Latin American Cats, Economic values and prospects. **'The World's Cats' Vol.3** No.1.

Koford, C. 1978. The welfare of the Puma in California. **Carnivore Vol.1** No.1.

Knowles, J.M. 1980. Housing and breeding of big cats at Marwell. In Bardzo, J. (Ed.), **Proceedings of ABWAK Symposium 4.** ABWAK, Bristol.

Kralik, I. 1967. Breeding the Caracal Lynx at Brno Zoo. **International Zoo Yearbook 7:** 132.

Krishne-Gowda, C.D. 1967. A note on the birth of Caracal Lynx at Mysore Zoo. **International Zoo Yearbook 7:** 133.

Krishne-Gowda, C.D. 1968. A note on the behaviour of mating Tigers at Mysore Zoo. **International Zoo Yearbook 8:** 63 - 64.

Kunc, L. 1970. Breeding and rearing the Northern Lynx at Ostrava Zoo. **International Zoo Yearbook 10:** 83 - 84.

L

Law, G. and Boyle, H. 1983. Breeding the Geoffroy's Cat, *Felis geoffroyi,* at Glasgow Zoo. **International Zoo Yearbook 23:** 191 - 194.

Lawrence, R.P. 1980. Cats at West Midland Safari Park. In Bardzo, J. (Ed.), **Proceedings of ABWAK Symposium 4.** ABWAK, Bristol.

Leslie, G. 1973. Breeding Scottish Wildcats at Aberdeen Zoo. **International Zoo Yearbook 13:** 150.

Leyhausen, P. 1962. Smaller cats in the zoo. **International Zoo Yearbook 3:** 11 - 21.

Leyhausen, P. 1979. **Cat Behaviour.** Garland Press, New York.

Leyhausen, P. 1980. The preservation of Felid species: can captive breeding be the answer? In Bardzo, J. (Ed.), **Proceedings of ABWAK Symposium 4.** ABWAK, Bristol.

Leyhausen, P. and Falkena, M. 1966. Breeding the Brazilian Ocelot cat in captivity. **International Zoo Yearbook 6:** 176 - 178.

Leyhausen, P. and Tonkin, B. 1966. Breeding the Black-footed Cat in captivity. **International Zoo Yearbook 6:** 178 - 182.

Louwman, J.W.W., and Van Oyen, W.G. 1968. A note on breeding Temminck's Golden Cat at Wassenaar Zoo. **International Zoo Yearbook 8:** 47 - 48.

Lucas, G. 1980. Housing of cats in Europe. In Bardzo, J. (Ed.), **Proceedings of ABWAK Symposium 4.** ABWAK, Bristol.

M

MacDonald, T. 1971. Postscript. **Dinny's Digest.**

MacGregor, W. 1978. The status of the Puma in California. **The World's Cats. Vol.3** No.1.

Manton, V.J.A. 1970. Breeding Cheetahs at Whipsnade Park. **International Zoo Yearbook 10:** 85 - 86.

Manton, V.J.A. 1971. A further report on breeding Cheetahs at Whipsnade Zoo. **International Zoo Yearbook 11:** 125 - 126.

Manton, V.J.A. 1974. Birth of a Cheetah to a captive bred mother. **International Zoo Yearbook 14:** 126 - 129.

Manton, V.J.A. 1975. Cheetah breeding at Whipsnade Park: A report on the first seventeen births. **International Zoo Yearbook 15:** 157 - 160.

Manton, V.J.A. 1980. A half-century of home bred Cheetahs. In Bardzo, J. (Ed.), **Proceedings of ABWAK Symposium 4.** ABWAK, Bristol.

Marma, B.B., and Yunchis, V.V. 1968. Observations on the breeding, management and physiology of the Snow Leopards at Kaunas Zoo. **International Zoo Yearbook 8:** 66 - 74.

Maruska, E.J. 1976. Reported in **AAZPA Newsletter. XVIII, No.9:** 20.

Matola, S. 1984. In **Wildlife magazine, August** 398 - 399.

Mayo, J.G. 1967. Tranquillisation of a male Snow Leopard for Semen extraction. **International Zoo Yearbook 7:** 148 - 150.

McBride, C. 1981. **Operation White Lion.** Collins, London.

McClure, R.C., Dallman, M.J., and Garrett, P.G. 1973. **Cat anatomy: An atlas, text and dissection guide.** Lea and Febiger, Beckenham.

McCord, C.N. 1974. Courtship behaviour of free ranging Bobcats. **The World's Cats. Vol. 2.**

McDougall, C. 1977. **The face of the Tiger.** Rivington Deutsch.

Mellen, J.D., Stevens, V.J. and Markovitch, H. 1981. Environmental enrichment for Serval, Indian Elephants, and Canadian Otters at Washington Park Zoo, Portland. **International Zoo Yearbook 21:** 196 - 201.

Meyer-Holzapfel, M. 1968. Breeding the European Wildcat at Berne Zoo. **International Zoo Yearbook 8:** 31 - 37.

Miller-Ben-Shaul, D. 1963. The composition of milk of wild animals. **International Zoo Yearbook 4:** 333 - 342.

Miller, P. 1977. Hold that Tiger. **Dinny's Digest.**

Moore, J.A. 1970. Some notes on the climatic adaptability of large cats in captivity. **International Zoo Yearbook 10:** 144.

Moore, T. 1980. Conservation of the genus Felis. In Bardzo, J. (Ed), **Proceedings of ABWAK Symposium 4,** ABWAK, Bristol.

Morris, D. 1965. **The Mammals.** Hodder and Stoughton, London.

Morse, R.W. and Follis, T.B. 1974. Physiological normal research in Lions. **'The World's Cats' Vol.2.**

Murphy, E.T. 1976. Breeding the Clouded Leopard at Dublin Zoo. **International Zoo Yearbook 16:** 122 - 124.

Myers, N. 1975. **The Cheetah in Africa.** I.U.C.N.

Myers, N. 1976. **The Leopard in Africa.** I.U.C.N.

Myers, N. 1978. The status of the Leopard and Cheetah in Africa. **'The World's Cats' Vol.3** No.1.

N

Nardelli, F. 1983. Clouded Leopards. **Howletts and Port Lympne News**.

Nowak, R.M. and Paradiso, J.L.1983. **Walker's Mammals of the World.** 4th Edition. The John Hopkins University Press, London.

O

O'Grady, R.J.P. 1980. Melanism in breeding Wild Cats. In Bardzo, J. (Ed.) **Proceedings of ABWAK Symposium 4,** ABWAK, Bristol.

P

Paintiff, J.A. and Anderson, D.E. 1980. Breeding the Margay at New Orleans Zoo. **International Zoo Yearbook 20:** 223-224.

Pennycuick, C.J. and Rudnai, J. 1970. A method of identifying individual Lions with an analysis of the reliability of identification. **Journal of Zoological Society of London.**

Perry, R. 1970. **The World of the Jaguar.** David and Charles, Newton Abbot.

Petersen, M.K. 1974. Preservation of wild felids by captive breeding **'The World's Cats' Vol.2.**

Petersen, M.K. 1977. Courtship and mating patterns in Margays, **'The World's Cats' Vol.3** No.3.

Petersen, M.K. 1978. Growth rates and other post-natal developmental changes in Margay. **Carnivore Vol.1** No.1.

Petersen, M.K. 1979. Behaviour of the Margay. **Carnivore Vol.2 No.2.**

Poelker, R. 1978. Status and management of the Puma in Washington. **'The World's Cats' Vol.3 No.1.**

Povey, R.C. and Davis, E.V. 1977. Panleukopaenia respiratory virus infection in wild felids. **'The World's Cats' Vol.3 No.3.**

Q

Quillen, P. 1981. Hand-rearing the Little Spotted Cat. **International Zoo Yearbook 21:** 240 - 242.

R

Rawlins, C.G.C. 1972. Cheetahs in captivity. **International Zoo Yearbook 12:** 119 - 120.

Reiger, I. 1979. Scent rubbing in carnivores. **Carnivore Vol.2 No.1.**

Ricciuti, E.R. 1979. **The Wild Cats.** Windward Books, Leicester.

Rich, M.S. 1982. Siberian Lynx. **Zoonooz.**

Richardson, D. 1982. Jungle Cats. **Howletts and Port Lympne News.**

Richardson, D. 1985. Management of Siberian Lynx at Howletts Zoo Park. **International Zoo News** 14 - 17.

Richardson, D. 1985. A management protocol for breeding Clouded Leopards. Personal Communication.

Robinson, R. 1979. Cytogenetics of the living Felidae. **Carnivore Vol.2 No.2.**

Rodriguez de la Fuente, et al. 1971. **World of Wildlife.** Orbis Publishing, London.

Rudnai, J. 1975. How Lions communicate. **SWARA Vol.2 No.6.**

Rudnai, J. 1979. Activity rhythm of a free ranging Lion population. **Carnivore Vol.2 No.2.**

Ryden, H. 1982. The cat that walks alone. **Wildlife magazine.** July.

S

Sadleir, R.M.F.S. 1966. Notes on reproduction in the larger Felidae. **International Zoo Yearbook 6:** 184 - 186.

Sankhala, K.S. 1967. Breeding behaviour of the Tiger in Rajasthan. **International Zoo Yearbook 7:** 133 - 147.

Sankhala, K.S. 1978. **Tiger.** Collins, London.

Sayer, A. 1982. **The St. Michael encyclopedia of the cat.** Octopus Books Ltd. London.

Schaller, G.B. 1967. **The deer and the tiger.** University of Chicago Press, Chicago.

Schaller, G.B. 1972. **The Serengeti Lion. A study of predator-prey relations.** University of Chicago Press, Chicago.

Scheffel, W. and Hemmer, H. 1975. Breeding Geoffroy's cat, *Leepardus geoffroyi salinarum,* in captivity. **International Zoo Yearbook 15:** 152 - 154.

Schurer, U. 1978. Breeding Black-footed Cat in captivity. **Carnivore Vol.1** No.2.

Shorey, D. and Eaton, R.L., 1974. Management and behaviour of the Bengal Tiger under semi-natural conditions. **'The World's Cats' Vol.1.**

Silveira, E.K.P.da. 1972. A case of cannibalism amongst ocelots in Brasilia Zoo. **International Zoo Yearbook 12:** 182 - 183.

Singh, A. 1982. The death of a tigress. **Howletts and Port Lympne News.**

Skeldon, P.C. 1973. Breeding Cheetahs at Toledo Zoo. **International Zoo Yearbook 13:** 151 - 152.

Smith, R.M. 1978. Movement patterns and feeding behaviour of Leopards in the Rhodes Matopos National Park. **Carnivore Vol. 1** No.3.

Smithers, R.N. 1977. The Serval-A spotted cat. **Flora and Fauna No.30.**

Smithers, R.N. 1978. The regal Caracal. **Flora and Fauna No.33.**

Smuts, G.L., 1978. Effects of population reduction on the travels and reproduction of Lions in Kruger National Park, **Carnivore Vol.1** No.2.

Smuts, G.L., Hanks, J. and White I.J. 1978. Reproduction and social organization of Lions from Kruger National Park. **Carnivore Vol.1** No.1.

Smuts, G.L., Robinson, G.A. and White, I.J. 1980. Comparative growth of male and female Lions. **Journal of Mammalogy.**

Speidel, G. 1975. The Siberian Tigers in the Milwaukee County Zoological Park. **Der Zoologischer Garten.**

Staples, M. 1979. The Geoffroy Cat. **Zoo Life.**

Stehlik, J. 1971. Breeding Jaguars at the Ostrava Zoo. **International Zoo Yearbook 11:** 116 - 118.

T

Thomas, W.D. 1965. Observations on a pair of Cheetahs at Oklahoma City Zoo. **International Zoo Yearbook 5:** 79 - 82.

Thompson, R. and Landreth, H.F. 1974. Reproduction in captive Cheetahs. **'The World's Cats' Vol.2.**

Tomkies, M. 1977. **My wilderness wildcats.** MacDonald, London.

Tong, J.R. 1974. Breeding Cheetahs at Beekse Bergen Safari Park. **International Zoo Yearbook 14:** 129 - 130.

Tonkin, B.A. 1972. Notes on longevity in three species of Felid. **International Zoo Yearbook. 12:** 181 - 182.

Tonkin, B.A. and Kohler, A. 1978. Breeding the African Golden Cat in captivity. **International Zoo Yearbook 18:** 147 - 150.

Tonkin, B.A. and Kohler, A. 1981. Observations on the Indian Desert Cat. **International Zoo Yearbook 21:** 151 - 154.

U

Ulmer, F.A. 1941. Melanism in Felidae with special reference to the Genus Lynx. **Journal of Mammalogy.**

Ulmer, F.A. 1966. Voices of the Felidae. **International Zoo Yearbook 6:** 119 - 120.

Ulmer, F.A. 1968. Breeding Fishing Cats, *Felis viverrina*, at Philadelphia Zoo. **International Zoo Yearbook 8:** 49 - 55.

V

Vellat, C. 1971. Birth of three Cheetahs at Montpelier Zoo. **International Zoo Yearbook 11:** 124 - 125.

Van Aarde, R.J., and Blumenberg, B. 1979. Genotypic correlates of body adrenal weight in a population of feral cats. **Carnivore Vol.2 No.4.**

Van Den Brink, F.H. 1967. **A Field Guide to the Mammals of Britain and Europe.** Collins, London.

Van Hoof, J.A.R.A.M. 1965. A large litter of Lion cubs. **International Zoo Yearbook 5:** 116.

Vaneysinga, C.R. 1969. The dietary requirements of Lions, Tigers and Jaguars when kept outdoors in the winter months. **International Zoo Yearbook 9:** 164 - 166.

Vaneysinga, C.R. 1970. A note on keeping Cheetahs under winter conditions. **International Zoo Yearbook 10:** 144 - 146.

Veselovsky, Z. 1967. The Amur Tiger in the wild and in captivity. **International Zoo Yearbook 7:** 210 - 215.

Veselovsky, Z. 1970. The breeding biology of the Siberian Tiger. **Der Zoologischer Garten.**

Veselovsky, Z. 1975. Notes on the breeding of Cheetah at Prague Zoo. **Der Zoologischer Garten.**

Visser, J. 1978. The status and conservation of the smaller cats of southern Africa. **'The World's Cats' Vol.3** No.1.

Volf, J. Breeding the European Wildcat at Prague Zoo. **International Zoo Yearbook 8:** 38 - 42.

W

Wackernagel, H. 1968. A note on breeding the Serval Cat, *Felis serval,* at Basel Zoo. **International Zoo Yearbook 8:** 46 - 47.

Waller, R. 1972. Tiger Census - How it was done. **Oryx.**

Wayre, P. 1969. Breeding the European Lynx at the Norfolk wildlife Park. **International Zoo Yearbook 9:** 95 - 96.

Wasser, S.K. 1978. Structure and play in the Tiger. **Carnivore Vol.1** No.3.

Widholzer, F.L. et al. 1981. Breeding the Little Spotted Cat. **International Zoo News.**

Wrogeman, N. 1975. **Cheetah under the sun**. McGraw Hill, Johannesburg.

INDEX

African Golden Cat	65
African Wild Cat	9
albinism	44, 115, 121, 125, 131, 138
anal gland	2
Andean Cat	95
Ant-hill Tiger	23
barking	17, 45
Bay Cat	71
Black-footed Cat	22
Black Panther	115
Bobcat	44
Caffer Cat	9
Caracal	32
Cheetah	138
Chinese Desert Cat	26
Clouded Leopard	106
dentition	1, 2
Domestic Cat	13
ears	2
European Lynx	36, 41
European Wild Cat	4
Fishing Cat	58
Flat-headed Cat	63
flehman	2
Fossa	74
Geoffroy's Cat	86
Harvard Law of animal behaviour	23
Head rubbing	14, 108
Hyoid	2, 106, 113, 139
Iriomote cat	61
Jacobson's organ	2
Jaguar	121
Jaguarundi	73
Jungle Cat	19
King Cheetah	138
Kodkod	90
Leopard	115
Leopard Cat	52

Lion	131
Little-spotted Cat	84
Lynx	
manes	135, 139
man-eating	117, 123, 127
Manul	49
Marbled Cat	103
Margay	80
melanism	19, 28, 32, 44, 68, 84, 86, 90, 92, 115, 121, 125, 138
nictitating membrane	50
nomads	99, 127, 132, 134
non-retractible claws	24
nose-leather	3
Ocelot	76
Oncilla	84
Onza	144
Ounce	110
Pallas's Cat	49
Pampas Cat	92
Panther	see Leopard
peri-oral glands	2
pooking	128
prides	132
prusten	111, 128
Puma	97
pupil, of the eye	106, 139
purring	45, 113, 128, 173
Reed Cat	19
Rusty-spotted Cat	56
Sand Cat	16
Serval	28
Servaline	28
Snow Leopard	110
Spanish Lynx	41
Swimming	53, 77, 122
tapetum	1
teeth	1, 2
Temminck's Cat	68, 71
Tiger	128
vibrissae	1
Viverridae	74